T0065675

WEAPONS

▨ OF ▨

CHESS

♟ ♟ ♟

AN OMNIBUS
OF CHESS STRATEGY

by

Bruce Pandolfini

A FIRESIDE BOOK
Published by Simon & Schuster

Fireside

Rockefeller Center
1230 Avenue of the Americas
New York, New York 10020

Designed by Irving Perkins Associates
Manufactured in the United States of America

30 29 28 27 26 25   Pbk.

Library of Congress Cataloging in Publication Data

Pandolfini, Bruce.
    Weapons of chess : an omnibus of chess strategy / by Bruce
Pandolfini.
        p.   cm.
    ''A Fireside book.''
    Includes index.
    1. Chess.   I. Title.
    GV1449.5.P37   1989
    794.1'2—dc20   89-34925
                                                    CIP

ISBN-13: 978-0-671-65972-1
ISBN-10:   0-671-65972-3

CONTENTS

✝ ♞ ✝

For Faneuil Adams

ACKNOWLEDGMENTS

I would like to thank Carol Ann Caronia, Bruce Alberston, Idelle Pandolfini, Larry Tamarkin, Doug Bellizzi, Mark Levine, and Burt Hochberg from the world of chess, and Renée Rabb, Bonni Leon, Sean Devlin, and Laura Yorke, my editor, from Fireside.

ABOUT THE AUTHOR

BRUCE PANDOLFINI is the author of ten instructional chess books, including *Bobby Fischer's Outrageous Chess Moves, Principles of the New Chess, Pandolfini's Endgame Course, Russian Chess, The ABC's of Chess, Let's Play Chess, Kasparov's Winning Chess Tactics, One-Move Chess by the Champions, Chess Openings: Traps and Zaps,* and *Square One.* He is also editor of the distinguished anthologies *The Best of Chess Life, Volumes I and II.* Perhaps the most experienced chess teacher in North America and the Executive Director of the Manhattan Chess Club, Bruce Pandolfini lives in New York City.

INTRODUCTION

♟ 🛡 ♟

Weapons of Chess is mainly about strategy, with emphasis on the middlegame. Strategy means abstract thinking and planning, as opposed to tactics, which are the individual operations used to implement strategy. Tactics are specific; strategy is general. Tactics tend to be immediate, strategy long-term.

Weapons of Chess is a book of concepts and practical advice. It defines and explains the key motifs of strategic play. It is concerned more with thinking than with specific moves. It presents plans, elucidates their formulation and execution, and emphasizes pawn play over brilliant combinations. It helps a player answer the question: What do I do now?

The book is divided into thirty-eight essays, arranged alphabetically by theme-title for ease of use. For example, if you are interested in learning about doubled pawns or have recently encountered them in a game, you can turn to the section entitled "Doubled Pawns" in this book, where you will find a brief definition and descriptions of doubled pawn types (double pawns are either connected or isolated), followed by a discussion of their ramifications. Many essays include illustrative diagrams focusing on the essay's important themes.

The essay format permits several features to stand out almost at once. Since there are no variations of chess moves to wade through, you can actually read the text without a board and pieces. You may enjoy setting up the positions on a real chessboard for reinforcement, but this is not necessary. *Weapons of Chess*, presents abstract chess themes without relying on chess notation. A knowledge of the algebraic names of squares is helpful, but even this is not required. Every idea is explained in words.

Another advantage of this book is its simple, yet thorough tapestry of concepts, plans, practical advice, and basic do's and don'ts. If you're a teacher, your students will absorb some of these general rules much more easily than they do intricate sequences of chess moves, and the clear presentation should immediately improve the students' level of play. Most books on chess strategy are so blurred with complicated variations and options that they confuse more than elucidate. *Weapons of Chess* clears the air with the dictum that things "tend" to be such and such but may not always be so. In other words, it encourages thinking. You don't have to memorize moves.

Understanding the pawn world, particularly that world's clandestine implications, is the basis of sound planning. Even when dealing with themes about pieces, the book relates them to pawn structure.

At the heart of many problems is the isolated pawn, which, though often weak and immobile, is sometimes surprisingly resilient. This double aspect is best exemplified by the "isolated d-pawn," the most common subject of strategy in the book. Because of its plus-and-minus duality, and because it is so involved in many of the difficulties students encounter in creating chess positions and constructing plans, four different headings have been devoted to it.

Even if you are mainly interested in only one of the four aspects of the d-pawn, you will derive great benefit from reading about all of them. This principle holds for some of the other essays too. Some points of strategy are discussed in more than one section. You may want to turn to those sections that relate to a strategy you are reading about at the moment. To this end, associated listings are given in the Related Section Index for your convenience.

Supplemental terms are defined briefly in a glossary. In the context of broader discussions, it is helpful to have these minor terms clarified and at your fingertips. Here, they are presented alphabetically, so that you can find them when you need them.

No book on chess strategy can be exhaustive, nor should it be. But *Weapons of Chess* contains everything of practical value for the casual chessplayer. The entries "Analysis" (how to analyze), "Calculating Variations" (how to calculate), "Oversights" (how to avoid them), and "Visualization" (how to see moves in your head) should be most rewarding. Read the book all the way through, or turn to it selectively, whenever you need it, as you would any tool. For that is what a chess book should be: a tool.

A WORD ON CHESS NOTATION

You need not know how to record a chess game in order to read *Weapons of Chess,* though I recommend that at some point you learn to do so. What you need to know now are the algebraic names of the squares. For that purpose:

- The board is regarded as an eight-by-eight grid with sixty-four squares.
- The *files* (the eight vertical rows of squares) are lettered *a* through *h*, beginning at White's left.
- The *ranks* (the eight horizontal rows of squares) are numbered *1* through *8*, beginning with the row closest to White.

You can readily identify any square by combining its letter and number, with the letter written first (see Diagram A). For example,

A
An algebraic grid

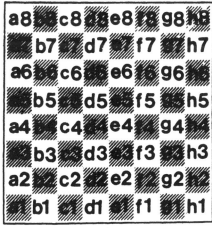

Black

a8 c8 e8 g8
b7 d7 f7 h7
a6 c6 e6 96
b5 d5 f5 h5
a4 c4 e4 g4
b3 d3 f3 h3
a2 c2 e2 g2
b1 d1 f1 h1

White

the square occupied by White's King in the original position is *e1*, and the original square for Black's King is *e8*. All squares in the algebraic grid are always named from White's standpoint.

If at first you have trouble remembering where all the squares are, I suggest you make a photocopy of the diagram above and use it as a bookmark while reading *Weapons of Chess*. Thus it will always be handy when you need it, though after a while you probably won't need it at all. As a further reference point, note that in this book the numbers and letters of all the positions are conveniently arranged on the outside of each diagram.

RELATED SECTION INDEX

♟ ♞ ♟

Many of the main subjects in *Weapons of Chess* are related and overlap, though they may be in different parts of the book. Although it is not necessary to read related sections together, doing so may reinforce the material and help you remember it better.

In the index below, all main sections are arranged alphabetically. Under each main heading appear related sections.

11

ADVANTAGE

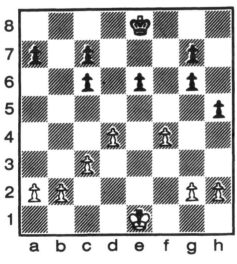

Any factor that increases your winning chances is an advantage. The player who has the most such factors in his or her favor has the advantage in the game; that is, the better winning chances.

Specific advantages fall into categories. For instance, if you have fewer weaknesses than your opponent, you probably have an advantage in pawn structure. In Diagram 1, since White's pawns are in fewer groups than Black's, they are easier to guard. Black's pawns have more weaknesses.

1
White has the better pawn structure

TIME

If you have more pieces developed than your opponent, you probably have an advantage in time. White has a large edge in development in Diagram 2.

2
White has a big edge in time

Note that White has one less pawn than Black. In order to capture the White b-pawn, Black wasted valuable time and moved the queen several times. As a result, Black now has only three developed pieces, while White's seven pieces are all in action. This gives White a winning superiority in time.

SPACE

Control of the center, more advanced pawns, rooks on open and half-open files—these are some indicators of an advantage in space. In Diagram 3, White's spatial edge is significant.

MATERIAL

If you have more men or more valuable men than your opponent, you have an advantage in material. In Diagram 4, White has an extra pawn but Black has a rook compared with White's knight. Black therefore has a slight material advantage.

3

White controls more space than Black

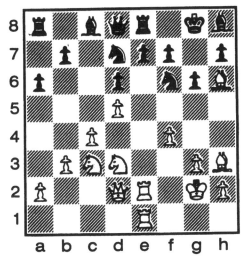

4

Black is ahead in material

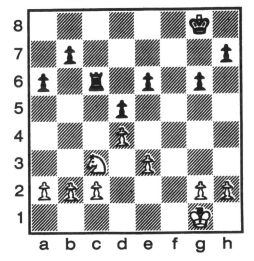

SAFETY

If your king is less exposed than your opponent's, you probably have an advantage in king safety. In Diagram 5, White's king is securely castled. Black's is stuck in the center and dangerously exposed.

5
White's king is safer than Black's

TYPES OF ADVANTAGES

Advantages can be temporal, positional, or material. Temporal advantages might include: faster piece development or having been able to force your opponent to make extra pawn moves (instead of developing pieces). Temporal advantages have a way of evaporating, so they should be converted to other types of advantages early in the game. Your opponent will be able to catch up in development (for example) if you don't make something of your early development soon enough.

Positional advantages, such as control of the center, good pawn structure, controlling open or half-open files, and obtaining a safe position for the king, change constantly throughout the game. When you play positionally, you are trying for small advantages—and sometimes your opponent either doesn't realize what you are doing or doesn't consider those advantages important. But although those little advantages may not amount to much individually, when they're accumulated and cultivated, they can eventually add up to a real positional superiority. To neutralize these advantages your opponent may have to surrender material or submit to a strong attack on his king.

Material advantages, such as trading a knight for a rook, or a queen for two minor pieces, keeping a good bishop, or trading a bad bishop are usually the most decisive.

Advantages in material and pawn structure tend to be more permanent than temporal advantages. If you have an extra pawn, unless something radical happens you will probably still have it ten moves later. Thus, some advantages are more useful, practically speaking, while others are harder to turn into a win.

ANALYZING THE COMPETITION POSITIONALLY

Try to build your game and increase your overall advantages. Reduce the weaknesses in your own position and increase those in your opponent's. To do this, you must be able to evaluate correctly. You must know how to analyze a chess position.

ANALYSIS

Analyzing a chess position is like making a mental tally sheet of the weaknesses and strengths for each side. You determine the game's character and potential by imagining possible moves and responses, by looking for your opponent's threats and finding threats of your own.

While playing, divide the analytic process into two sections: When it is your move, be concrete and specific. When it is your opponent's move, let your mind wander over the board, and ask yourself general questions about the position.

QUESTIONS ARE THE KEY

The key is to ask questions. Suppose your opponent has just played and now it's your move. You must analyze specifically and directly.

First you might ask: What does my opponent's move threaten? Are any of my pieces or pawns attacked and threatened? If so, are they adequately protected? If they aren't, what can I do to safeguard them?

If a piece is threatened, probe the position to determine whether you should guard your piece, move it to safety, or trade it for an enemy unit of equal value. Perhaps you can negate the threat by making a more significant threat of your own.

DON'T IGNORE ENEMY THREATS

But be careful. If you try to meet your opponent's threat by making a threat of your own, and your opponent is able to defend against your threat with an additional threat, you will then be faced with *two* threats on the next move. It might not be possible for you to meet both of them.

For example, in Diagram 6, Black could make a terrible blunder.

6
Black should move the threatened knight

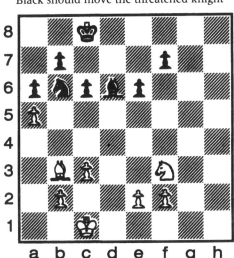

Black should simply move the knight to safety. But what if Black, seeing the possibility of inserting a check at f4 with his bishop, decides to postpone dealing with the threat for one move? See Diagram 7.

Black thinks that White must deal with this check and therefore can't carry out the threat to the knight. But White answers the check by blocking it with the e3-pawn! Suddenly Black is faced with two threats: the original one to the knight and the new one to the bishop. Black will lose a piece on the next move.

7
Black's blunder costs a piece

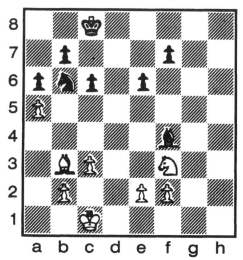

NOT THREATENED?

If you determine that your opponent poses no threats, then do some threatening of your own. Generally, you will want to threaten your opponent without risking your own game. You will also want to build your potential for future attack. You should not threaten just to threaten.

To some extent, your analysis will be based on what has gone before. Determine whether your previous threats have been met by your opponent's last move. If your opponent answered your last threat with a new threat of his own, decide which threat is more serious before choosing your next move.

WAITING FOR THE MOVE

While you are waiting for your opponent to move, you probably won't have to prepare an answer to an immediate threat, since you don't know what your opponent's going to play—maybe there won't even *be* a threat. But it's a good time to ask yourself general questions to fill out your picture of the position.

Does the enemy have any weaknesses? Given the opportunity, how could they be exploited? What are the enemy's strengths? Are there any potential threats the enemy can generate? What are *my* weaknesses? Can I get rid of them? Can I compensate for them?

DEVELOP YOUR SYSTEM

It isn't necessary to ask these specific questions. You may compose your own questions that may be more effective for you. The point is to develop your knowledge of the position by asking yourself questions and answering them. That's the way to analyze a chess position.

Once you're involved in a game, you may be able to draw upon your previous considerations to facilitate and expedite your analysis. You don't have to repeat the analysis on every move.

But remember that the purpose of analysis is to determine a course of action. *First* analyze the position, *then* make a plan or decide on your next move. You can't plan for the future if you don't know where you stand now.

ANTI-POSITIONAL MOVE

♟ ♜ ♟

An anti-positional move is one that is unsound strategically. It differs from a blunder, which is an error or oversight that loses a piece or pawn.

An anti-positional move violates the logic or direction of the game. Usually, it is a pawn move that weakens a key square or group of squares.

An example of an anti-positional move would be to castle and then make the king vulnerable by moving the pawns that are shielding it. Creating these weaknesses in the castled fortress is anti-positional.

In Diagram 8, White has no significant Kingside weakness.

8
White to move

ATTACKS AREN'T EVERYTHING

Most anti-positional moves are made for the sake of attack. But attacking for the sake of attacking, without regard to the consequences, creates weaknesses.

If, in Diagram 8, White tried to dislodge Black's knight by moving the pawn from g2 to g4, he would create irreparable weaknesses at f3, f4, h3, and h4. Those are squares the g-pawn could never again protect once it moved to g4.

Black would answer such an anti-positional move by transferring the knight to f4 (Diagram 9). At f4 the knight attacks White's queen and endangers White's weakened kingside.

9

White has permanent kingside weaknesses

PAWNS CAN NEVER GO HOME

Avoid frivolous pawn moves that attack for the sake of attacking. Threaten if you will, but make sure there is a sound reason for every pawn move. *Pawns can never retreat.* Once a pawn moves past a square, it can never guard it again. Enemy pieces can occupy such weak squares.

Since you're going to be stuck with every pawn thrust you make, make sure you understand the consequences of a pawn move before you make it. If you don't, it's probably a bad idea.

BACKWARD PAWN

♟ ♟ ♟

A backward pawn is one that cannot be advanced with the support of a friendly pawn or protected by one. Although it isn't physically prevented from moving, it can't advance because it would be captured by an enemy pawn on an adjoining file. Its inability to move safely makes it a weakness in its owner's position and a target for attack, as in Diagram 10.

PROTECTING THE BACKWARD PAWN

Diagram 10 shows a backward black pawn on the b-file.

10
Black's b6-pawn is backward

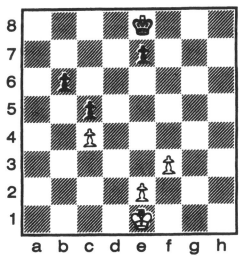

The b6-pawn cannot advance because White's c4-pawn could then win it. But if Black's king were in position to guard b5 (which it could do if it stood on c6), and if White's king were not also guarding b5, the pawn could advance safely.

Note, in Diagram 10, that White's c4-pawn actually holds back two pawns—not only Black's backward pawn at b6, but Black's pawn at c5, which can't move at all.

SUBJECT TO ATTACK

A backward pawn is subject to attack by the enemy queen and rooks along the half-open file in front of it. (A half-open file is one occupied by pawns of only one color.) The half-open file facilitates queen and rook attacks because this long-range artillery is not blocked by its own pawns.

In Diagram 11, both White and Black have backward pawns, at b3 and b6, respectively. Neither pawn is in real danger, however, because the b-file is blocked and can't be used by the enemy's rook.

11
Neither backward pawn can be attacked along
the b-file

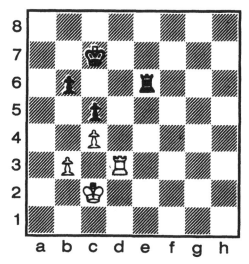

MAKING YOUR OPPONENT SUFFER

When a pawn is backward and subject to attack along the half-open file in front of it, the defender's entire game may suffer, as in Diagram 12.

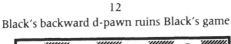

12
Black's backward d-pawn ruins Black's game

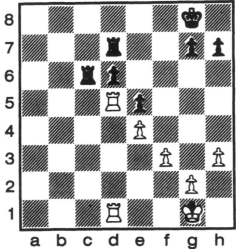

In Diagram 12, Black's backward d6-pawn is attacked by two white rooks and defended by two black rooks. But Black's need to protect that weak pawn has given White a fine tactical opportunity—to win the e-pawn!

The e5-pawn seems protected well enough by the d-pawn, but the d-pawn is actually pinned. If it moves off the d-file, the black rook right behind it on d7 will be seized by a white rook. This allows White to capture the e5-pawn with the rook on d5. If Black takes the White rook on e5 with his d-pawn, then White's other rook takes Black's rook at d7. If Black doesn't take the rook, White will move the rook from e5 to safety on the next move, staying a pawn ahead. In either case, White comes out a pawn to the good.

A MORE RESILIENT ROOK

13
White has the advantage but cannot force a win

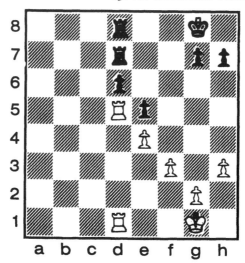

Diagram 13 is the same as Diagram 12 but with Black's rook transferred from c6 to d8. This more resilient placement averts the white rook's capture on e5, because Black's rook at d7 is now protected. White still has positional superiority, though, because his rooks have greater freedom of action while Black's are tied to defense.

PILING UP ON THE WEAKNESS

In Diagram 14, Black holds on to the d-pawn for now, but White with the move can advance the e-pawn to e5, attacking the backward d6-pawn a third time. The d6-pawn could not then capture

14
White piles up on the backward pawn

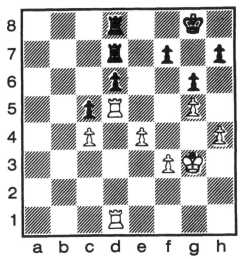

on e5 because if the pawn deserted the d-file, Black would lose his rook at d7. No matter what reasonable defense Black tries after White plays e4-e5, White gains a pawn on the next turn, capturing on d6 with his pawn from e5.

EVERYONE JOINS IN

Other pieces can join the attack against a backward pawn. In Diagram 15, White's rooks are supplemented by a queen, a bishop, and a knight, all attacking d6.

In Diagram 15, Black's d6-pawn is attacked five times, by all of White's pieces except the king. It's also defended five times, by Black's queen, rooks, bishop, and knight. White's game is fully active, Black's solely defensive. Moreover, with Black's kingside weaknesses, the position is ripe for a breakthrough sacrifice.

If it is White's move, advancing the e-pawn to e5 breaks through the position. Black would either have to capture White's pawn on e5 or face the distasteful chore of defending both d6 and f6.

15
Black's position is totally passive

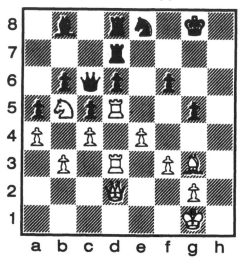

16
After White's pawn advances to e5

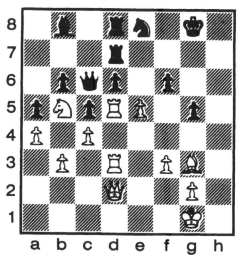

If Black takes White's e-pawn with the d-pawn, the rook on d7 falls to White's triple attack: two rooks and queen. If Black captures the e-pawn with the f-pawn instead, White's queen can take on g5 or his bishop, exploiting the same d-file pin, can safely capture on e5 (Diagram 17). And now Black's g5-pawn is unprotected and menaced and the kingside ripped open.

17
Black's position is in ruins

THE FRONT LINE

The square immediately in front of a backward pawn can be a big problem because it is vulnerable to enemy occupation. This occupation can be powerfully effective, since the occupying piece can't be chased away by a pawn. Diagram 18 shows a knight in that fortunate position.

Evaluating this position, we see that Black has a bishop while white owns a knight. A bishop is generally considered to be slightly stronger than a knight, but this case demonstrates the exception. Entrenched at d5, White's knight is a tower of strength, and black cannot drive it away.

18
The knight is strong on d5

In fact, if it is White's move he can win the backward pawn on d6. First, White exchanges the knight for the bishop, capturing on e7 with check. After Black takes back on e7 with the rook, White's rook captures the now unprotected d6-pawn.

The tactic of driving away a defending piece or removing it by capture is called undermining. White, in Diagram 18, actually dealt with both of the d-pawn's defenders at once. The bishop was captured by the knight, and the rook was diverted from the d-file by having to recapture on e7.

ADVANCING THE PAWN

Sometimes the particular features of a position allow the backward pawn to be advanced even when there isn't sufficient protection for it. Diagram 19 gives such a case.

Black to move can rid himself of the backward d-pawn simply by advancing it to d5. Whichever way White takes it—with the knight on c3, the pawn on c4, or the pawn on e4—Black has a tactical resource: The bishop on e7 goes to c5, pinning White's rook on e3 to its king on g1. After White protects the rook by moving the king from g1 to f2, Black will take the rook with the bishop.

19
Black can advance his d-pawn

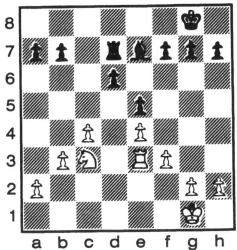

These transactions have cost Black the d-pawn but gained a rook for a bishop. Giving up a minor piece (a bishop or a knight) for an enemy rook is known as winning the exchange. Trading a rook for a knight or a bishop is losing the exchange.

Of course, if it is White's turn to move in Diagram 19, the knight invades to d5, and Black's backward pawn can't advance. White will then have time to reposition the rook and king. This should allow White to retain a slight edge. Strategy is often dependent on tactics.

PUSHING AHEAD

Other tactical opportunities may make it possible to get rid of a positionally weak backward pawn. Diagram 20 provides an illustration.

20
Black can get rid of his backward d-pawn

In this position, Black to move can push the d-pawn, even though it is not supported by protectors. White could not then capture it with the e4-pawn, for Black would then follow with a thrust of his own e-pawn, from e5 to e4. Double threat! White's knight at f3 is attacked by Black's e-pawn, and both white rooks are skewered by Black's g7-bishop along the a1-h8 diagonal. White must lose material.

BRINGING IN THE TROOPS

Another way to alleviate a backward pawn weakness is to bring a friendly pawn to an adjacent file by capturing an enemy. Then the backward pawn might be advanced with the help of that supportive pawn. Diagram 21 exemplifies this situation.

White has just captured a black knight on c6, and Black has two ways to take back—with either the c8-rook or the b7-pawn. Capturing with the rook leaves Black saddled with a backward pawn at d6. This pawn will then be subject to attack.

By taking with the b7-pawn, Black drives away White's remaining knight, and makes it possible for the d6-pawn to advance later with the protection of the pawn on c6.

21
Black should capture on c6 with the b-pawn

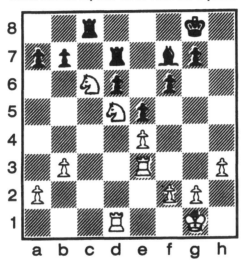

If you can get rid of a weakness by making a clever pawn capture—as in this example, in which a distant pawn was relocated to support a backward friend—do it. And when attacking an opponent's pawn weakness, try to avoid exchanges that eliminate that weakness or improve the enemy pawn structure.

KNOCKING OFF THE FOE

Sometimes you can prepare to advance a backward pawn by exchanging off the enemy pawn that is preventing its advance. This is shown in Diagram 22.

Black can eliminate the backward d-pawn problem by advancing the f-pawn from f7 to f5.

If White takes Black's f-pawn with the e-pawn, Black's bishop recaptures on f5, attacking the rook at b1. And when White's rook moves to safety, Black takes the b-pawn with his b4-rook.

22
Black can eliminate White's e-pawn

If White doesn't capture on f5, Black's f5-pawn can capture White's e4-pawn, which is attacked also by the b4-rook. White, of course, as well as Black, has pawn weaknesses in this example: the isolated pawns at b2 and e4.

MAKE IT A SAFE OCCUPATION

The enemy pawn is clearly backward and you, the attacker, have a firm grip on the square in front of it. You can occupy that square with a piece, especially a knight, and that seems like an excellent idea. But before you do it, make sure that if your piece is captured there, you will be able to take back with another piece, not a pawn. The reason will be clear in Diagram 23.

23

White should occupy the d-file with a rook before
moving his knight to d5

It would be a mistake to play the knight immediately to d5. Black would take the knight with the bishop, and White would be forced to take back with a pawn. That would close the d-file to White's rooks, and thus eliminate White's ability to attack the backward pawn. In fact, it would no longer be a backward pawn.

The correct procedure for White in Diagram 23 is first to play a rook, perhaps the one on f1, to d1. This gains time because it attacks the backward pawn at d6. It also adds protection to d5. After Black defends the d6-pawn with a rook, White *then* could move the knight to d5. If Black should capture the knight, White would take back with the rook instead of a pawn. The d-file would remain clear for White's rooks as a channel to attack the d6-pawn.

GOOD ADVICE

Try to avoid accepting backward pawns. But if you do get saddled with one, try to trade it for a healthy enemy pawn or to develop counterplay that prevents your opponent from attacking your weakness. This might mean exchanging pieces so that the half-open file in front of the backward pawn becomes blocked by an enemy pawn.

In harassing an enemy backward pawn, first control the square in front of it with your own pawns and pieces. When suitable, try to occupy that square with a piece, particularly a knight. But if that piece is captured, be sure you can take back with another piece; otherwise you might lose the ability to attack the backward pawn.

BAD BISHOP

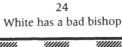

A bad bishop is one that is blocked or impeded by its own pawns, which are fixed on the same color squares traveled by the bishop. A light-square bishop is bad if its pawns are stuck on light squares, and a dark-square bishop is bad if its pawns are fixed on dark squares.

RESTRICTED BY ITS OWN PAWNS

24
White has a bad bishop

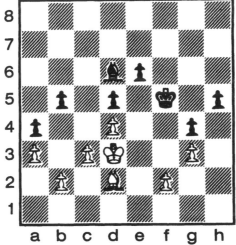

In Diagram 24, the mobility of White's dark-square bishop is hindered by its own pawns. Black, on the other hand, has a good bishop that is unhampered by any of its pawns. In fact, Black's bishop and pawns complement each other: The bishop guards the dark squares, the pawns guard the light squares.

In Diagram 25, Black has a bad bishop, and because of it he loses the game.

25
Black to move loses

Black's bishop is bad because its mobility is hindered by its own pawns at b5 and f5. White's bishop, contrariwise, is good, its pawns not fixed on squares of its own color.

Black to move must lose a pawn. Black can move either his king or bishop. If the bishop moves, Black loses whichever pawn is left unprotected. If Black moves his king, White's king intrudes on the vacated area: c5 if Black's king moves to e6, and e5 if Black's king moves to c6. Whichever pawn White's king is able to attack then falls.

FIX ENEMY PAWNS ON THE SAME COLOR AS THE BISHOP

It's foolish to think that the pawns belong on the same color squares as the bishop because the bishop can easily defend them there. That strategy simply leaves the other color squares completely undefended and causes severe weaknesses.

If you can, mess up your opponent by making him put his pawns on squares where they block his bishop. As for your own pawns, try to place them on squares of the other color than your bishop. This way, you can guard squares of both colors, avoid weaknesses, and let your bishop move freely.

STRATEGY SUMMATION

Avoid having your own pawns fixed on the same color your bishop uses, but try to fix your *opponent's* pawns on the same color squares occupied by *his* bishop. If you have a bad bishop, try to exchange it for your opponent's good bishop (or knight). If you have a good bishop, don't exchange it unless you have a good reason. If your opponent has a bad bishop, try to invade on the squares his bishop can't protect.

THE BIND

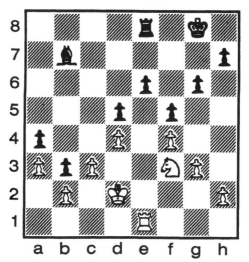

When one side's pawns and pieces are so well positioned that they prevent the enemy from moving freely, a bind is created. A player who is in a bind is not only cramped and unable to make freeing pawn moves but is also vulnerable to attack.

In Diagram 26, White has an unbreakable bind on the e5-square: The e6-pawn is frozen in place.

26
White has a bind on e5

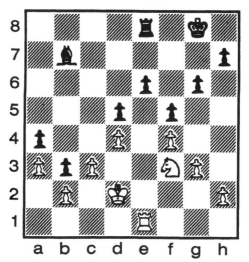

Pawns are often used to create a bind. In a variation of the Sicilian Defense called the Maroczy Bind, for instance, two centrally placed pawns effectively hinder the movement of enemy pieces (Diagram 27).

27
White has a bind on the square d5

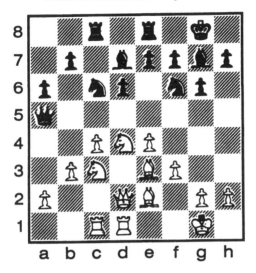

In the Maroczy Bind, White's pawns at c4 and e4 make it extremely difficult for Black to free his position by advancing the d-pawn to d5. As long as White can hinder that d-pawn advance, Black will have less space than White and a more restricted game.

Try to set up binds by using your pieces and pawns to restrict your opponent's freeing pawn moves. If you can keep the enemy cramped long enough, he may eventually be forced to make weakening or cumbersome moves that impair his position.

The key to using the bind successfully is to keep the bind tight until you can convert it into a tangible, permanent advantage. Release it too soon and your opponent may be able to equalize or even seize the initiative with a counterattack.

BISHOPS OF OPPOSITE COLOR

When Black and White have one bishop each, one controlling the light squares and the other the dark, they are said to have bishops of opposite color.

ENDGAMES ARE USUALLY DRAWN

Endgames with opposite-color bishops tend to be drawn, even if one side is ahead by a pawn or two, because the defending bishop

28
The opposite-color bishops draw

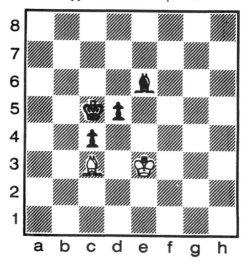

can usually blockade the enemy passed pawn or pawns. Since the attacking bishop doesn't control the same squares, the blockade is often unbreakable, insuring the draw, as Diagram 28 illustrates.

In this position, Black is two pawns ahead, and even though they are connected, the pawns are totally immobilized by the blockading White king and bishop. Black doesn't have sufficient force to push the d-pawn to d4. Black's light-square bishop guards the light squares, but d4 is a dark square, so Black's bishop is merely an idle bystander. White's bishop merely marks time moving along the a1-h8 diagonal, keeping watch on the d4-square, and Black has no way to make progress.

THE ATTACKER HAS THE ADVANTAGE IN THE MIDDLEGAME

Bishops of opposite color favor the defender in the endgame, but in the middlegame the reverse tends to be true—the attacker has the upper hand. Diagram 29 is an exemplary case.

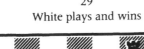

29
White plays and wins

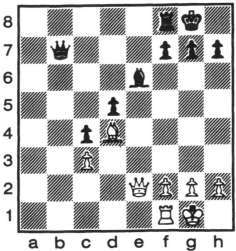

This diagram shows the advantage of opposite-color bishops during a middlegame attack. White's queen shoots to e5 where, backed up by the d4-bishop in an awesome battery, it threatens mate at g7.

How does Black stop the mate? The only way is to block the diagonal by moving the f-pawn to f6. Unfortunately, this leaves the bishop at e6 unprotected, and White's queen takes it for free.

In such situations, the defending bishop, moving on different-color squares than the attacking bishop, is unable to protect the attacked squares in front of its king. It's as if the attacker were playing with an extra piece.

WHAT'S GOOD EARLIER MAY BE BAD LATER

If you are behind by a pawn or two, try trading minor pieces so that you reach an endgame with bishops of opposite color. This gives you some chances of drawing, especially if you can blockade the enemy passed pawns. If you have an extra pawn or two, avoid exchanges that leave opposite-color bishops.

In the middlegame, if you and your opponent have different-color bishops try to use yours for attack. Your opponent may not be able to neutralize its power.

In the middlegame, these cases, the bishops often work in combination with other pieces to be effective.

BLOCKADE

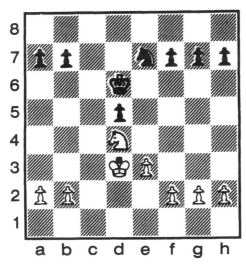

A blockade is the blocking of a passed or isolated pawn by an enemy piece, or the restraining of a pawn's advance by guarding and occupying the square in front of the pawn, also called the blockading square. Once the pawn is fixed by the blockade, a generalized attack can be launched against it.

In Diagram 30, White's knight blockades Black's d-pawn by occupying the d4 blockading square and preventing the pawn from moving. White's king and e3-pawn also guard d4.

30
White blockades Black's isolated pawn

OCCUPY THE SQUARE IN FRONT

Such a blockade—occupying the square in front of an isolated enemy pawn—is possible because there are no unfriendly pawns on adjoining files to prevent it. Since the blockading square can't be guarded by a pawn, the blockading piece has nothing to fear.

FIRST RESTRAIN

It makes good sense to restrain a pawn's advance before assailing it because it's easier to attack a sitting than a moving target.

Generally a pawn can be stopped from advancing by controlling the blockading square. And when you control it you can occupy it safely.

Diagram 31 shows the value of guarding the square in front.

31
White should restrain the d-pawn's advance

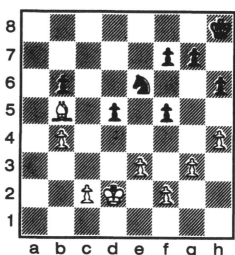

White's bishop eventually can attack Black's isolated d-pawn from f3 or from c6. But Black, by pushing the d-pawn, can force a trade with White's e-pawn, thus dissolving the weakness. From White's standpoint, it is better to guard d4 again, to prevent Black from getting rid of his weak pawn.

THEN ATTACK

White should play the c-pawn ahead one square, securing a firm grip on d4 and restraining Black's d-pawn. White can then position the bishop on c6. To protect the d-pawn, Black will have to retreat his knight to c7. White will follow by moving up his king to attack the d5-pawn again. Black will not be able to save it.

If you can't actually win the isolated pawn after blockading it, you will probably at least be able to force your opponent's pieces into defensive roles.

BLOCKADERS: THE GOOD AND THE BAD

Occupying the blockading square with a piece is optimal in most cases. Some pieces are particularly effective as blockaders. Knights, for example, can function beautifully in front of an isolated or passed pawn. The knight blocks the pawn's advance without reducing its own mobility, since it can jump over all obstacles.

32
Black's knight blockades

The use of Black's knight as a blockader in Diagram 32 is a good example of how this works.

Black's knight is an excellent blockader here, where it prevents White's d-pawn from moving and is also ready for action. Notice that if White's king tries to dislodge the knight, White loses a pawn: If the king attacks from e4, the knight checks on c3 and wins the pawn on a2. If the king attacks from c4, the knight checks on e3, winning the g2-pawn.

BISHOPS AS BLOCKADERS

Bishops are reasonably good blockaders, too. A bishop can blockade an enemy isolated pawn while maintaining attacking potential along its two diagonals and also guarding the immediate approach squares so the enemy can't break the blockade.

Diagram 33 illustrates the bishop's powerful placement.

33
Black's bishop is a fine blockader

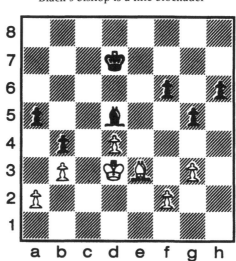

ROOKS DON'T MAKE IT

Rooks tend to be the worst blockaders, because their mobility can be restricted in a blockading position. Consider Diagram 34. White to play can force a draw even though Black has an extra rook.

34
White breaks the blockade

White forces a draw by moving the king to d7 (or b7). Black will have to sacrifice the rook to stop the pawn (or capture it when it reaches the 8th rank). Afterward, White's king can get back in time to draw.

Replace the rook with a Black bishop and White's king can't break the blockade. Diagram 35 shows that both d7 and b7, the approach squares, are guarded by the bishop.

35
White's king can't break the blockade

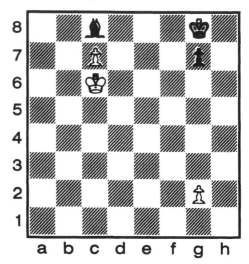

BLOCKADE TIPS

Try to blockade enemy passed and isolated pawns. Guard the blockade square with pieces and pawns and occupy it with pieces. In particular, aim to maneuver knights into blockade position.

If you have an isolated pawn and your opponent is attempting to blockade it, try to advance the pawn and exchange it for a healthy enemy pawn. If you have a passed pawn and the enemy is blockading it, try to drive away the blockader so your pawn can move ahead.

BLOCKED CENTER

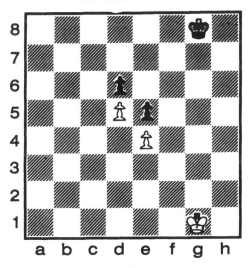

The center is blocked when the pawns belonging to both Black and White allow little or no movement in that part of the board. With movement in the center difficult or impossible, play proceeds either on the flanks or along the c- and f-files, just off center.

CLOSED CENTER

Diagram 36 shows a type of blocked center known as a closed center.

In this type of center, activity must be created just off center, on the c- and f-files.

36
The center is closed

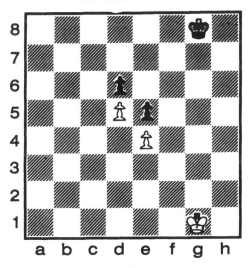

In Diagram 37, White should be trying to advance the f-pawn to f5, attacking the base of Black's pawn chain. (See the chapter "Pawn Chain.") Conversely, Black should go for White's base at d4 by moving the c-pawn to c5.

37
The action moves to the f-file and the c-file

THE STONEWALL

In a stonewall formation the center is incompletely blocked; each side usually has one square in it that can be occupied by a knight and guarded by two pawns.

In Diagram 38, White's stonewall pawns at d4, e3, and f4 face off against Black's stonewall at d5, e6, and f5. Both White and Black have a center pawn that can move, although if White's e3-pawn or Black's e6-pawn advanced it would be captured and lost immediately.

Since e4 is doubly guarded by Black pawns, it makes an excellent base for a Black knight. White doesn't have a pawn to guard e4 and keep a Black knight out. The square corresponding to e4 for occupation by a White knight is e5.

38
A double stonewall

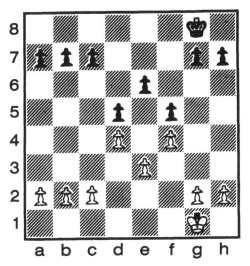

Diagram 39 shows strong knight placements in a stonewall blocked center.

39
Stonewall knights in a blocked center

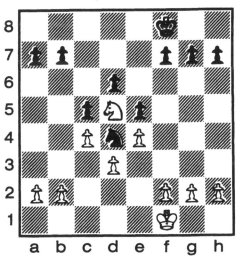

To develop play against stonewall formations, try to make undermining pawn advances on the c- and f-files just off center. In Diagram 37, White should be trying to advance the c-pawn to c4. Black should be trying to advance the c-pawn to c5.

In Diagram 39, White should be trying to move his f-pawn to f4; Black should be trying to move his f-pawn to f5.

BREAKTHROUGH COMBINATION

A breakthrough combination is a series of moves in which a passed pawn decides a chess game. Handled correctly, the pawn can become a new queen or force the opponent to surrender material to stop it. And an advantage in material can eventually lead to checkmate.

FASHIONING A PASSED PAWN OUT OF NOTHING

When you don't already have a passed pawn, sometimes you can create one by a breakthrough sacrifice or combination.

Diagram 40 shows the most famous type of breakthrough combination. If White goes first, he can make a new queen by force.

PUSH THE MIDDLE PAWN

The key is to start by pushing the middle pawn to g6. Black must take this pawn, for if he doesn't it will capture either Black's f- or h-pawn and become a new queen on the next move.

If Black captures with the h-pawn, toward the center, then White moves the f-pawn to f6, offering another sacrifice.

40
White makes a new queen with a breakthrough combination

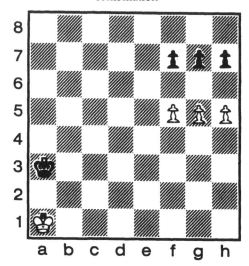

41
White has created a passed h-pawn

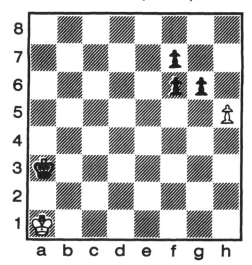

This, too, must be accepted, or White's f6-pawn will capture Black's g7-pawn and become a new queen. After Black's g7-pawn takes on f6, we have the position shown in Diagram 41. White's h-pawn is free to move up to h6, queening in two more moves.

If, after White's g-pawn moves to g6, Black captures the g-pawn with the f-pawn, away from the center, White moves his h-pawn to h6, forcing Black's g7-pawn to capture the h6-pawn (Diagram 42). Suddenly White has a passed f-pawn that will turn into a queen at f8 in three moves.

42
White has created a passed f-pawn that will queen in three moves

BREAKING THROUGH WITH A PIECE SACRIFICE

Sometimes a passed pawn can be created by sacrificing a piece instead of a pawn. Though the price is greater, the result can be the same: a pawn promotes to a new queen. Diagram 43 illustrates.

43
White sacrifices a bishop to create a passed pawn

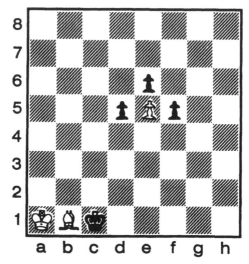

The winning idea is to capture Black's f-pawn with the bishop. If Black takes the bishop with the e-pawn, White's e-pawn pushes on to become a new queen. If Black doesn't take the bishop, it will capture the e6-pawn, and the e5-pawn becomes a queen anyway.

Breakthrough combinations are most effective when the pawns are far advanced because the enemy king or other defending pieces may not have time to stop the passed pawn from promoting or to organize a defense.

CALCULATING VARIATIONS: HOW TO DO IT IN YOUR HEAD

♟ ♙ ♟

My students often ask me how good players calculate variations in their heads. There is no easy answer to this question, but it helps to structure your thinking to avoid tactical oversights later in the game.

When it's your move, do you play the first idea that comes into your head? You shouldn't. Unless you have no choice, you should consider other possibilities. On the other hand, analyzing too many moves wastes time—and is really a fruitless task anyway.

Whether you are responding to your opponent's last move, formulating a plan, or combining defense with counterattack, you undoubtedly will need to evaluate several possible moves. Let's call these possible moves candidates.

As you scan the board for candidates and review your thoughts from previous turns, various ideas will suggest themselves. Rather than analyze any of these in depth, first make only a cursory initial review of the potential moves. If any seem worth further consideration, put them on a mental list. You should be able to find three or four candidate moves for this list unless there is a forced move to make, such as a recapture.

Avoid the temptation of analyzing in depth the first move you think of. That could be a serious procedural error. One reason is that you may be wasting your time analyzing an unworthy move. If you first frame several moves into a list and mentally examine them, you may find that one or two of the moves are clearly more attractive than the others. This reduces your workload by eliminating moves not worth analyzing *before* you analyze them.

The mental list serves another function. Arrange the possible moves on it in order of potential strength and consider the most promising move first. If it involves long analysis and even then is still murky, remember that there are other candidate moves to consider. If you had not created that mental list you might forget that there were other moves to analyze. It is hard to start looking for alternatives after you've already spent some time analyzing. But your mental list helps you keep your thoughts in order.

In summary: (1) make a superficial analysis of move possibilities; (2) create a mental list of the candidate moves; (3) arrange those moves in order of preference, eliminating those not worth serious thought; (4) analyze the first move on your list as deeply as you can; (5) if you run into trouble, turn to the next candidate on the list.

This process may not enable you to analyze like World Champion Garry Kasparov. And it won't equip you to calculate ten or fifteen moves in your head (few people can). But it may help you see and calculate more deeply than you do now. It's only a structure on which you can improve.

DOUBLED PAWNS

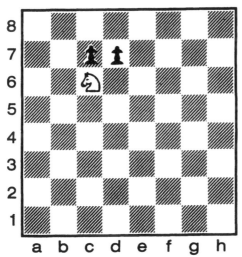

Two pawns of the same color that occupy the same file (the result of a capture by one of them) are called doubled pawns.

CONNECTED OR ISOLATED

In Diagram 44, doubled c-pawns will be created when Black's d-pawn captures White's knight.

44
Black gets doubled c-pawns

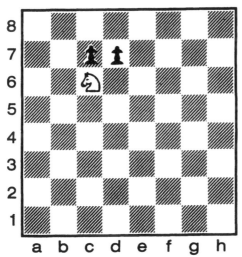

Doubled pawns may be connected or isolated. Connected doubled pawns have at least one friendly pawn occupying an adjacent file. This pawn could be an important protector for the doubled pawns.

A DOUBLED PAWN CAN BE YOUR FRIEND

In Diagram 45, for example, Black can save the doubled c5-pawn from the c1-rook's threatened capture by defending it with the adjoining b-pawn, moving it to b6.

45
Black's b-pawn can protect the c-pawn

Doubled pawns can be isolated, without a friendly adjacent pawn to offer protection. Such pawns are separated from friendly pawns by at least one file, or they lie along the board's edge.

In Diagram 46, Black has isolated doubled pawns on the b- and h-files. Similarly, White has doubled pawns on the d- and g-files.

Doubled pawns tend to be unfavorable because they can be weak, difficult to defend, or subject to enemy attack, especially if they are immobile. But if they can't be attacked, they aren't necessarily weak. Not realizing that, chess novices often go out of their way to avoid doubling their pawns, even to the extent of marring

46
Four pairs of doubled isolated pawns

their position in other ways. Just remember that doubled pawns aren't necessarily disastrous. Weigh the good and bad points of the exchange that creates them to make an objective decision.

But there are times when doubled pawns do lead to tactical problems, such as when they expose your king's position. They also may result in an unfavorably unbalanced pawn structure in which the enemy can derive a winning pawn majority on one side or in one sector of the board.

DOUBLED PAWNS MAY LEAD TO AN ISOLATED PAWN

Moreover, a side effect of doubled pawns is often the isolation of another friendly pawn, as in the exchange leading to the doubled pawns shown in Diagram 47.

In this position, Black's doubled c-pawns resulted when a White knight moved from d4 and was traded for a Black knight on c6. When White captured Black's knight, Black took back on c6 with the b7-pawn.

47
An exchange on c6 has created an isolated Black
a-pawn

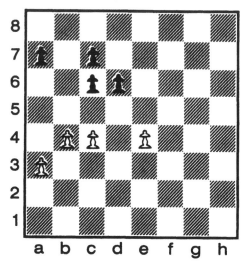

Those doubled c-pawns are not necessarily bad for Black, unless White can successfully attack and exploit them. In fact, by bringing the b7-pawn to c6, Black has increased his strength in the center: suddenly the key d5-square is guarded by the c6 doubled pawn. Now White can't safely occupy d5 with a knight or any other piece.

On the other hand, the exchange has created an isolated a-pawn that can no longer be guarded by one of its brothers. If the a-pawn is ever attacked, Black will have to defend it with a piece, which then becomes rather passive. Furthermore, with the b7-pawn having moved to c6, the squares a6 and a5 can no longer be guarded by a Black pawn and may become vulnerable to occupation by White pieces.

A BREACHED WALL

Some tactical problems involved in accepting doubled pawns are illustrated in Diagram 48.

White is saddled with doubled f-pawns, a result of the exchange of a Black knight on g5 for a White knight on f3. To avoid losing material, White had to recapture with the g2-pawn, which ended up on f3. This has seriously compromised the White king's position, for the g-pawn is no longer shielding the king.

48
Black moves and wins White's queen

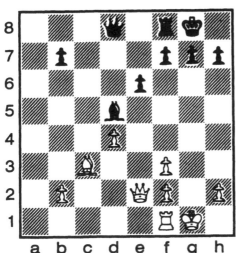

Black can capitalize on the gap immediately, moving his queen from d8 to g5, giving check. After White's king escapes to h1, Black's queen creeps to g4, attacking White's f3-pawn. The f3-pawn, pinned to White's king at h1 by the bishop at d5, can't escape.

Once Black's queen and bishop together bear down on the f3-pawn, White must sacrifice his queen to stop mate, because Black's bishop will capture the f3-pawn with check, setting up a mate threat at g2.

DOUBLED PAWNS AND PAWN MAJORITIES

An exchange that yields doubled pawns can also lead to the creation of a winning breakthrough or pawn majority. This is shown in Diagram 49.

49
White exchanges and breaks through

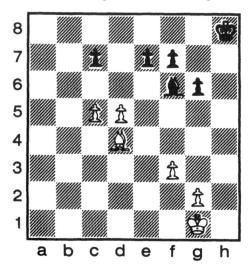

In this position, White wins by first exchanging bishops on f6. White captures Black's bishop with check, and Black recaptures with his e7-pawn, doubling the f-pawns.

White now has a winning imbalance: a queenside majority of two pawns to one. He can push through his d-pawn, protected by the c5-pawn, and make a new queen in a few moves. (Or White could first move the c-pawn to c6, then advance the d-pawn. Depending on Black's response, either White's c-pawn or d-pawn must queen.)

The doubled pawns in this example were not in themselves a problem. But with the e7-pawn drawn out of position, White gained a winning pawn advantage on the c- and d-files.

TO DOUBLE OR NOT TO DOUBLE

Should you ever permit the doubling of your own pawns? Is it ever an advantage to accept them?

Sometimes there is no practical choice—you accept either doubled pawns or some other disadvantage, such as loss of time or material.

In Diagram 50, for example, if White's knight captures Black's h6-bishop, giving check, Black has no choice but to take back with his g7-pawn. If he doesn't, for fear of exposing his king's position, and instead moves his king to the corner, White will then retreat his knight to safety, remaining a piece ahead.

50
White doubles Black's pawns

Which is worse, to slightly weaken your king's position or to lose a knight? Most of the time, losing a knight means certain defeat, while accepting a busted pawn structure may still allow considerable resistance—in fact, you might not even lose at all!

ALLOW IT OR BE MATED!

Sometimes an absurd example points out a logical fallacy, as in Diagram 51.

51
Should Black avoid doubled pawns or mate White?

It is Black's move. White threatens, whenever feasible, to capture Black's bishop on c6 with his knight. To keep material equality, Black would have to take back on c6 with the pawn on d7, accepting doubled c-pawns. Should Black avoid this by moving the bishop out of the range of White's knight?

Or should Black give checkmate by moving his knight from g5 to h3?

The correct answer, obviously, is to give mate! But in many almost equally obvious examples, a player fails to look at every aspect of the position and plays as if the opponent's threat is the only consideration.

Scrutinize the position carefully. It may contain a possibility that dwarfs the drawbacks of your opponent's potential threat.

ACCEPTING DOUBLED PAWNS

One reason to accept doubled pawns is to obtain an open file for your rook to exploit, as in Diagram 52.

Black's last move, the advance of the a-pawn from a5 to a4, assailed White's knight at b3. White could move the b3-knight out of attack, perhaps to d2.

52
Black doesn't fear the doubled f-pawns

In pushing the a-pawn, Black wasn't worried that White would play an in-between move and capture the knight on f6 with the bishop before moving the knight to safety. Though capturing the f6 knight forces the doubling of Black's f-pawns and the isolation of Black's h-pawn, it also opens the g-file for occupation by Black's rooks, meaning that White would be faced with two threats, not just one. The knight on b3 would still be attacked, and mate along the g-file would also be threatened by a Black rook moving to g8.

PURSUE YOUR OWN GAME

As you see, sometimes you may want to put off responding to enemy threats in order to implement an idea of your own. But if you decide to postpone defending for a move or two, make sure that after your opponent responds to your idea, you will still have enough time to answer his original threat. Take special care to see that the response to your in-between move will not add new threats. You might not be able to handle two threats with a single move.

There may be many reasons to allow the weakening of your pawn structure, but the only good ones give you advantages that outweigh any weaknesses you incur.

Remember: Isolated doubled pawns tend to be weaker than connected doubled pawns because, if attacked, they must be guarded by pieces. But sometimes doubled isolated pawns can be quite useful, as in the next example.

BEWARE TACTICAL THREATS!

53
White's doubled c-pawns guard key squares

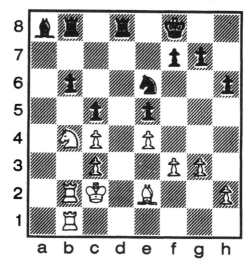

In Diagram 53, Black's last move was to advance the c-pawn from c6 to c5—a tactical error that leads to the loss of a pawn. White's knight leaps from b4 to d5, unleashing a triple attack against Black's beleaguered b6-pawn.

Black has no adequate way to save the pawn. It can't be sufficiently protected, and if Black captures the knight with the bishop on a8, White will straighten out his pawn formation by recapturing with his c4-pawn. Black will then have to guard against two threats: the double-rook attack on his b6-pawn, and the d-pawn's attack on the e6-knight. Because the knight is more important and must be saved, Black's b-pawn falls.

Of significance in this variation is that White's other c-pawn (c3) guards the possible invasion point d4. Were it not for that pawn, after White's c4-pawn captures on d5, Black's knight on e6 could move to d4 with check, gaining enough time to salvage the position.

So, even without Black's blunder—the pawn move c7-c5—White still has a positional edge because of his doubled and isolated c-pawns. The one on c4, in conjunction with the one on e4, anchors the White knight on d5 beautifully. And the pawn on c3 controls d4, preventing Black's knight from assuming an aggressive central post.

GOOD ADVICE

To sum up, doubled pawns often tend to be weak. Sometimes, they might even constitute a chronic or tactical weakness. In some situations, however, their existence is inconsequential or even advantageous.

Learn to take either side of the bet. If you see a way to saddle your opponent with doubled pawns, consider carefully whether they will be a liability or an asset. Be sure they won't help the enemy afterward.

If the resulting situation would be unclear, play in a manner that would increase the likelihood that the doubletons will remain a long-term weakness.

For yourself, try to avoid accepting doubled pawns if you can determine that your position will suffer afterward because of them. But don't go out of the way to avoid them if analysis indicates that they don't matter very much in the big picture. You might make a significant gain in time or position by allowing them. You have to get to know this!

If you are suddenly afflicted with double pawns, make the best of the situation and try to turn them into a strength. Sometimes you can do this by using the pawns as battering rams to expose or weaken your opponent's position. In other instances, you might be able to occupy the resulting open file with a major piece, thereby gaining attack advantages.

Judge each situation on its own merits, not by arbitrary principles.

DOUBLED ROOKS

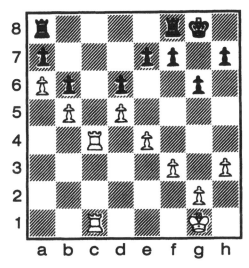

A player's rooks are doubled when both of them occupy the same rank or file. So aligned, the rooks protect each other and double the strength of their attack. In Diagram 54, White has doubled rooks on the c-file.

54
White's rooks are doubled on the c-file

White's doubled rooks protect each other and attack in tandem. Black can't neutralize White's grip on the c-file by placing a rook on c8 because White guards the square twice: with the c4-rook directly, and with the c1-rook in x-ray fashion, through the c4-rook.

Pieces lined up on the same rank, file, or diagonal constitute a battery. Doubled rooks, or a rook and a queen on the same rank or file, or a bishop and a queen on the same diagonal, are all batteries.

In Diagram 54, White's grip on the c-file gives him a positional advantage. White's plan should be to advance the front rook to the seventh rank, then to move it to another safe square on the seventh rank, and finally, if possible, to bring the other rook to the seventh rank as well. White's rooks would then be doubled on the seventh rank, a devastating battery.

BATTERING THE KING

Diagram 55 shows the power of a rook battery on the seventh rank.

55
White moves and mates in three moves

Black has a problem. His rook on f8 makes that potential escape square unavailable for Black's king. White forces mate by checking at g7 with the rook from c7. Black's king must go to h8. Then White's rook moves from g7 to h7, giving check again. Black's king scampers back to g8, and this time White's other rook, the one on b7, moves to g7, mating.

The doubled rooks on the seventh rank are just as impressive in Diagram 56.

56
White moves and mates in three moves

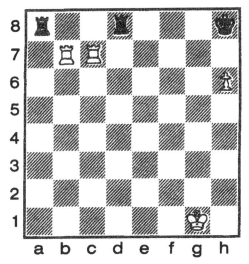

Though this time the f8-square is not blocked, the presence of the h6-pawn gives White another mating possibility. The game ends after White's rook checks on h7, Black's king moves out of the corner, White's b7-rook checks at g7, Black's king sidles to f8, and White's rook on h7 moves to h8, checkmate. Note that White's g7-rook is safe from capture because it is protected by the h6-pawn.

THE F8 VACANCY

The importance of keeping f8 vacant is critical in Diagram 57. White's winning move is king to e5, attacking the rook at f6. What should Black do? If he retreats the rook to f8, Black's king is deprived of a crucial escape square, and the White rooks mate with checks at h7 and g7. If Black's other rook moves from a8 to f8 to guard the f6-rook, White's rooks mate in the same way. So Black's rook at f6 is lost.

57
White moves and wins a rook

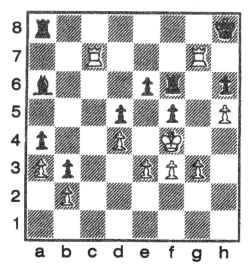

58
Black neutralizes White's control of the c-file

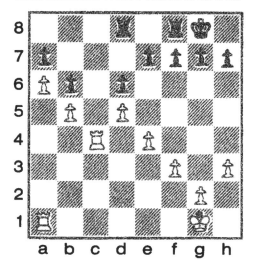

PREVENTIVE MEASURES

Generally, if you can prevent your opponent from doubling rooks on a file, you should. In Diagram 58, Black can do just that. Black neutralizes White's temporary control of the c-file by shifting his rook to c8. If White captures Black's rook, Black takes back with the other rook, taking over control of the c-file. If White doubles rooks instead, moving the a1-rook to c1, then Black answers by playing his rook from c8 to c5, preparing to double rooks himself. If White then exchanges rooks, Black is content to capture with a pawn, closing the c-file. Whatever happens, White's c-file grip evaporates.

ADVICE

Try to double your rooks on open and half-open files. Then move your rooks to the seventh rank, doubling them there if possible. Try to prevent your opponent from doubling rooks. You can usually do this by moving your rook to an open file on which there is an opponent's rook so that neither side controls the file exclusively.

EXCHANGING PIECES

An exchange is the capture of one of your opponent's pieces or pawns in return for one of your own. The units exchanged are usually of equivalent value—but not always.

If you capture an enemy rook with a rook of your own and your opponent takes your rook in turn, you have exchanged rooks. Since each rook is equivalent to about five pawns, it's an even trade.

If you capture the enemy queen and your opponent captures your queen, you have exchanged queens. Queens are worth about nine pawns each.

If you give up a bishop and gain one back, you have exchanged bishops. If you lose a knight and win an enemy knight, you have exchanged knights. bishops and knights are minor pieces worth about three pawns each. Even though bishops are preferred to knights in most positions, the two minor pieces are virtually equivalent. So if you give up a bishop but get a knight you have exchanged minor pieces.

TRADING UP AND DOWN

But if you give up a minor piece and gain a rook, you have not made an even exchange. You have won material! This is called winning the exchange. If you give up a rook and gain a minor piece, you have lost the exchange.

Obviously, if you lose a pawn and gain a pawn, you have made an even exchange. If you give up a bishop and get three pawns in exchange for it, this, too, is an even trade. But most of the time when we talk about trading or exchanging pieces, we mean queen for queen, rook for rook, minor piece for minor piece.

THE STRATEGY OF EXCHANGING

Exchanging pieces is often a factor in determining strategy. In the course of a game, circumstances develop in which exchanges become feasible. You will have to decide whether to make or avoid these possible exchanges, based on your analysis of the position and whether an exchange will improve or impair your situation. You should consider various critical factors.

In an endgame, you will want to trade if doing so will enable you to win by promoting a pawn, as in Diagram 59.

59
White has a winning simplification

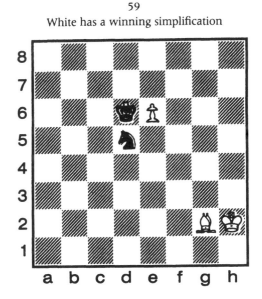

White could protect his attacked pawn by moving the bishop to h3, but Black's knight would then go to c7, capturing the pawn a move later. Instead, White takes the knight, and Black's king takes the bishop, a trade of minor pieces. But now White's e-pawn can advance to the queening square unmolested.

BEHIND BY A PAWN

In the endgame, if you are behind by a pawn or two, it is sometimes possible to reach a positional draw by exchanging pieces. Diagram 60 shows such a possibility.

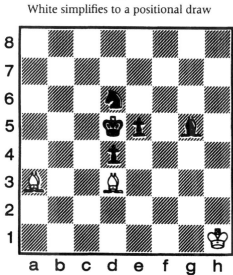

60
White simplifies to a positional draw

Black has some chances to win because of his two extra pawns. But White can prevent those pawns from moving safely by exchanging the a3-bishop for the knight. After Black's king takes back on d6, White's king goes to g2 and to f3 a move later. Black will then not be able to push either of his pawns without losing it, for White's king and bishop both guard the squares in front of the pawns.

SHOULD BISHOPS BE IDLE?

Black's bishop, meanwhile, can only watch idly. Since it is a dark-square bishop, it can't guard either e4 or d3, both light squares. The players have bishops of opposite color, which usually means a draw. A player with an inferior position should consider trading pieces if it leads to a drawn position based on opposite-color bishops.

WHEN NOT TO TRADE

If you want to increase the pressure, don't trade pieces if doing so would release the tension. Diagram 61 is an example of such a situation.

61
White to move. Don't exchange!

In this position, if White's d3-pawn captures Black's e4-pawn, Black's knight can take back, keeping the game equal in material.

But it's too soon to capture. First interposing the move bishop to a3 is stronger.

This move pins the Black knight and threatens to capture it for nothing. Black is compelled to defend the knight with the d-pawn, moving it to d6. White's bishop then takes the knight, and Black's d6-pawn takes back.

Now, finally, White's d3-pawn captures on e4. If Black's f5-pawn takes back, White's f2-knight makes the final capture on e4, putting White ahead by a pawn.

Thus, in Diagram 61, it is better to delay capturing on e4. That capture is much stronger after White improves his position.

TRADING IN TIME

Another reason to trade pieces is to gain time. Time is usually measured by initiative and development. You gain time by forcing your opponent to lose time or by completing an action in the fewest possible moves.

When you start an exchange, your opponent is usually forced to respond by taking back. This means that your opponent could not

62
White trades to gain time

proceed with his own plans, at least for the moment, and that it is again your turn to do what you want. For now, you have the initiative. (But remember, you may not want to capture first if it releases the pressure or if you have a better move instead.)

In Diagram 62, White's knight and g4-pawn are both menaced. White's knight is protecting the g-pawn. If White moves the knight to safety White will lose his g-pawn immediately. If White protects the knight with his king, Black will trade knights and then capture White's g-pawn with his h-pawn.

White can deal with the threats both to his knight and to his g-pawn with a gain of time by initiating the exchange of knights. After White's knight takes on c4, Black must take back to avoid material loss. White thus gains time to capture and win the h-pawn. Note that White could not take the h-pawn immediately because his knight was threatened.

LOSING TIME

Trading pieces doesn't always gain time. Sometimes it loses time, as in Diagram 63.

63
White to move. The bishop shouldn't take the
b8-knight

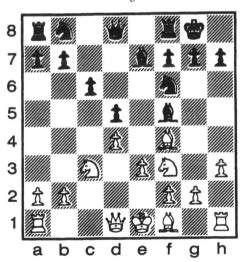

If White's f4-bishop captures the knight on b8, White loses time. To get to b8 to capture the knight, White's bishop will have used two moves (from its starting square on c1 to f4, then to b8). The knight didn't move at all, and now it never will. Black will have to recapture on b8, of course, probably with the a8-rook. So White has spent two moves to take the knight, Black only one to recapture—a net loss of one move for White.

But that's not all. Notice that in Diagram 63 both sides have developed three minor pieces and that Black has already castled. In Diagram 64, which shows the position after the exchange of bishop for knight, White has only two developed pieces, Black four! Thus the exchange was clearly a loss of time for White.

64
White has lost time

DON'T TRADE WHILE ATTACKING

If you have a menacing attack, you should avoid exchanges until the enemy is forced to make significant concessions or to yield concrete advantages, such as giving up material or weakening his pawn structure. The reason is that the number of threats closely corresponds to the size of the invading army, so careless trades can dilute your attacking chances. In Diagram 65, White shouldn't trade queens.

65
White to move shouldn't trade queens

White to move could trade queens here, but that would be a mistake. White's attack is strong enough to win the enemy queen or give checkmate—so why trade queens? By moving his queen to h3, for example, White threatens to win the rook at c8 and also to pin Black's queen along the g-file with his rook. So even though White is ahead materially and normally should trade pieces, here it makes more sense to avoid the trade and to press the attack.

You're on the opposite side of the coin when you're under attack. In such cases, you should seek trades to lessen the severity of your opponent's assault. In Diagram 66, Black can force a trade of queens and avoid mate.

White is threatening mate with the queen at either h7 or h8. Black can thwart this plan by checking at g5 with his queen. If White takes Black's queen, Black's bishop recaptures and mate is averted. If White doesn't take Black's queen, Black takes White's queen next move and the mate threat is stopped.

66
Black to move can stop mate

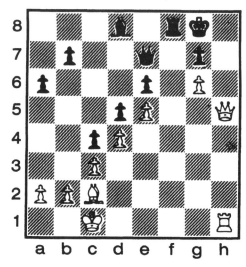

Trade pieces when under attack. With fewer pieces, it is harder to muster an attack. Especially try to trade off queens, the enemy's most potent assault force.

67
White should trade off a few pieces

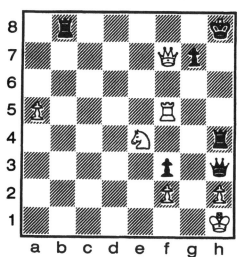

If there is a dominant principle about exchanging pieces, it is to exchange when ahead. Its logic is simple. By trading down when ahead you emphasize your material advantage. Ten units versus nine is proportionately less significant than two men versus one. In Diagram 67, White is threatened with four mates in one move: at h2, g2, f1, and b8.

How does White prevent all four threats? He trades pieces. First White's queen checks on f8. Black's rook naturally takes the queen, then White's rook takes back on f8, again with check, and Black's king must move up to h7, reaching the position of Diagram 68.

68
White regains the queen

Now White's knight checks at g5, and after Black's king moves out of check, the knight captures Black's queen on h3. And after Black's rook recaptures the knight (Diagram 69), White not only has avoided immediate mate, he has a winning endgame.

This principle—to trade when ahead—applies more to pieces than to pawns. When ahead in material, it's not usually a good idea to trade pawns. For example, when up a pawn, it would be a mistake to trade down to an ending of knight and pawn versus

69
White has avoided mate and has a winning endgame

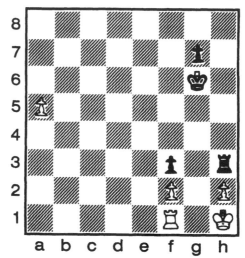

bishop if the bishop could sacrifice itself for the pawn. Although you would then be up a knight after your opponent's sacrifice, you wouldn't be able to win the game (king and knight versus king is a draw).

70
White to play has a winning game

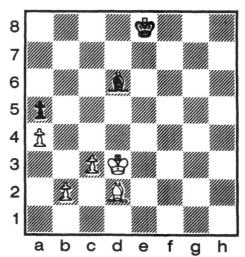

Diagram 70 shows a situation where offering an exchange of pawns would be the wrong strategy.

The correct strategy for White is first to attack the Black a-pawn with his king by moving it to b5, then, if necessary, maneuvering the White bishop to attack the a-pawn or to offer a trade of bishops.

The *wrong* idea is to move the b-pawn to b4, offering a trade of pawns and hoping to mobilize the connected pawns. Black will take White's b-pawn with the a-pawn, and White's c-pawn will recapture on b4 (Diagram 71).

CREATING A DRAW

71
Black to move sets up a positional draw

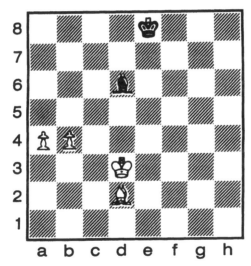

Black creates a drawn game by taking the b-pawn with the bishop. White's bishop recaptures and Black moves his king to d7, heading for the a8-corner. The game is drawn because White will be unable to drive Black's king out of the corner. The problem is that White's bishop can't control a8. This type of sacrifice, reducing to a positional draw, would have been impossible if White had kept all his pawns on the board. When ahead, don't exchange pawns, exchange pieces.

THE SHORT SIDE

If you are on the short side of the position—behind in material— the principles apply in reverse. Don't trade pieces, trade pawns. Maybe you'll have a chance to sacrifice down to a draw if you've systematically exchanged off pawns when possible.

FIANCHETTO

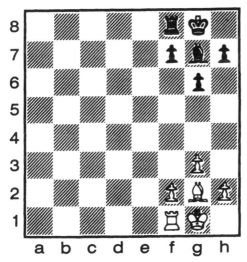

Fianchetto means the development of a bishop on the flank, usually on the second square of the b-file or g-file. Most fianchettos are on the kingside, where development of the king-bishop permits fast castling. Diagram 72 shows White's fianchettoed light-square bishop on g2 and Black's fianchettoed dark-square bishop on g7.

72
Each side has fianchettoed the king-bishop

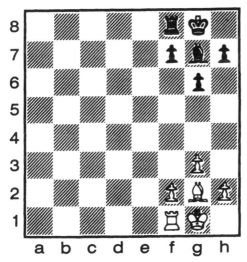

FIANCHETTO CAUSES WEAKNESSES

The chief problem with a fianchetto is that moving a knight-pawn to the third square on the file weakens the squares the pawn

93

was formerly protecting on the rook-file and the bishop-file. In Diagram 72, White's f3 and h3 are weakened, as are Black's f6 and h6.

Such weaknesses really become significant if the fianchettoed bishop is out of position or no longer on the board. In Diagram 73, Black to move mates White by jumping his knight from g5 to the abandoned h3 square. If White had a bishop at g2, or if his pawn were still at g2, this mate would be impossible because h3 would be guarded.

73
Black to move exploits White's weaknesses

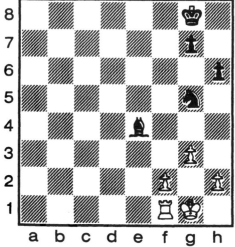

If you want to develop your bishop on the flank—which entails moving the knight-pawn on that side—try not to move the center-pawn on the same side too early. If you hold back the center-pawn, the third square on the bishop-file will have at least some pawn protection.

Further, you want to avoid wasting a move early in the game when time is critical. For example, consider the starting position. If White wants to develop his king-bishop from f1, he could start by moving either his e-pawn or his g-pawn. Moving both is unnecessary and wasteful. Unless required to by immediate circumstances, don't move both these pawns early. Save time and avoid weaknesses.

WHY DO IT?

Should you fianchetto? Certainly, if that's your preference. The opening setup you've planned on may necessitate it. You might also develop your bishop on the flank if you want to control squares of one color in particular. Then you would be playing either a light-square game or a dark-square game. In Diagram 74, for example, White controls the light squares and Black the dark squares.

74
White plays a light-square game, Black a dark-square game

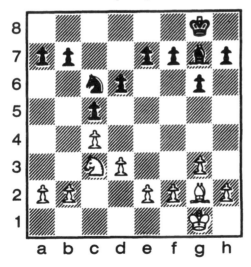

White's bishop, knight, and pawns at c4, d3, and e2 guard important light squares at d5, e4, and f3. Black's bishop, knight, and pawns at c5, d6, and e7 guard important dark squares.

There are many ways to undermine a fianchettoed position. One approach is to offer a bishop exchange on that side's third square on the rook-file, with the attacker usually backing up his bishop with the queen. If this invasion also blocks the enemy rook-pawn, and if you have not castled on that side, you may be able to push up your own rook-pawn, trade it off, and open a file for your rook on that side. Diagram 75 demonstrates.

75
Black can open the h-file by moving his h-pawn to
h5, then h4, then taking on g3

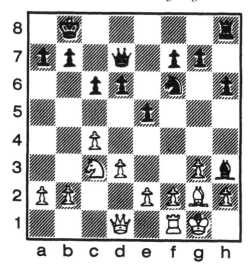

Black is offering a trade of bishops on h3. Now that White's h-pawn can't move, Black can advance his own h-pawn without hindrance to open the h-file for his rook.

WATCH OUT FOR TRAPS

There are all kinds of tricky tactics in such situations. Diagram 76 is an example.

Black has advanced his h-pawn to h5 and then to h4, where

76
Black has a winning sacrifice

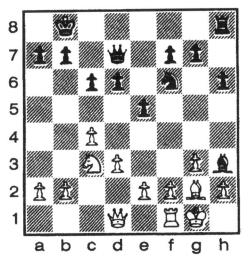

White's knight on f3 captured it. Although Black has given up a pawn, he has a crushing breakthrough combination.

First he captures the knight with his rook. White must take back with his g-pawn, to avoid loss of material. (If he declines the rook, it will retreat to safety, and Black will stay a knight ahead.) After the rook is captured, there's no longer a White pawn covering the g-file. Black's queen moves to g4, pinning the bishop at g2 and definitely giving checkmate next move.

If you intend to develop your bishop in a fianchetto, be aware of the possible consequences. Do not exchange off the fianchettoed bishop without a very good reason. If you do exchange, be sure the resulting weaknesses won't be too serious. Try not to flank your bishop if that side's center pawn has already moved. If you are assailing a fianchettoed position, try to exchange off the enemy king-bishop. It will then be easier to attack on that side.

FIXED PAWNS

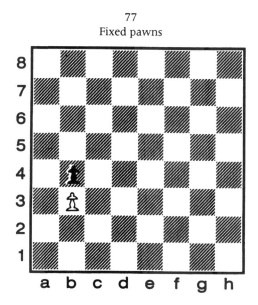

Pawns are said to be fixed when they are blocked by enemy pawns and rendered immobile. In Diagram 77, White's b3-pawn and Black's b4-pawn are fixed pawns. Each is blocked by the other and unable to advance.

77
Fixed pawns

When both fixed pawns occupy center squares, this is called a fixed pawn center. Diagram 78 shows such a formation.

Since a fixed pawn blocks and is blocked by an enemy pawn, neither can be attacked from the front by an enemy rook along the file it occupies. In Diagram 79, neither fixed pawn is susceptible to frontal attack. Each rook is blocked by its own pawn.

78
A fixed pawn center

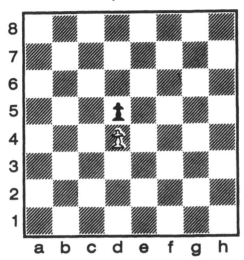

79
The pawns can't be frontally attacked along the e-file

FIXED STRONGPOINTS

Fixed center pawns guard two key squares, or strongpoints. A point or square is strong for you if your fixed pawn guards it. For each side, a fixed center's strongpoints are always on the center-file and the bishop-file next to it. In Diagram 80, White's strongpoints are c5 and e5. Black's are c4 and e4.

80
White's strongpoints are c5 and e5, Black's are c4
and e4

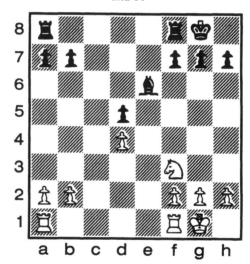

The basic plan for a fixed pawn center is to occupy the strongpoints. Once again, the knight is an excellent piece to do this. In Diagram 80, White's knight can move into e5 to assault Black's position. Black's bishop, given time and circumstance, might be able to occupy e4.

In Diagram 81, White is slightly better able to exploit the strongpoints.

81
White's strongpoints are stronger than Black's

DEFENDERS OF STRONGPOINTS

Overprotect the fixed pawn center's strongpoints, making sure they are as solid as possible. When you occupy a strongpoint with a piece, protect it with another piece so that the strongpoint will remain occupied by a piece.

Rooks are excellent strongpoint protectors in fixed centers. They guard key squares along the file they occupy. Moreover, rooks can offer support, even from a distance, where they are safe from enemy harassment.

Place your rooks on the open files leading to your strongpoints to control these squares more securely. In Diagram 82, White's rooks are placed properly, on the open c- and e-files, where they guard c5 and e5.

Don't move pawns indiscriminately. In Diagram 83, with fixed e-pawns, White has a distinct advantage. He is already occupying strongpoints with powerful pieces, and Black's pawns can't fight for control of these squares. For his part, Black doesn't occupy

82
White's rooks guard strongpoints

either of his potential strongpoints, and White can guard those squares (d4 and f4) with pawns, preventing Black from occupying them safely.

83
White's strongpoints are really strong; Black's are weak

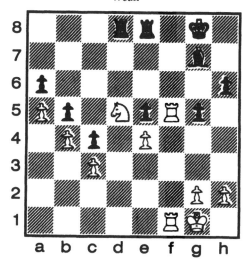

TOO FAR ADVANCED

In Diagram 83, Black's g5-pawn has advanced so far that it can't guard f5, so White's rook can occupy that square without being driven away. Black's c-pawn has also moved too far up the board, so it can't guard the other strongpoint, d5. Thus White's knight remains perched on d5.

Black's strongpoints aren't strong at all. Neither d4 nor f4 is occupied by a piece, and neither can be completely secured by Black. White's c3-pawn controls d4 equally with Black's e5-pawn. A Black piece moving to d4 would be captured and lost. Furthermore, White can guard f4, if necessary, by moving his g2-pawn to g3. Black simply has more weaknesses than White.

Try to retain the possibility of guarding the enemy's strongpoints with your own pawns. Make only necessary pawn moves.

THE KNIGHT SITS

Once a knight has occupied a strongpoint based on a fixed center, it may be difficult to dislodge, even if the defender has a

84
If Black moves the f-pawn, e6 is weakened

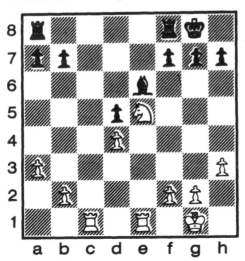

pawn to do it with. Diagram 84 gives an idea of the type of weakness such a defensive pawn advance entails.

If Black tries to drive away White's knight by advancing the f7-pawn to f6, the e6-square is weakened. White's rook can then attack it, as well as the bishop sitting on that square, once the knight moves to safety.

ENDGAME PROBLEMS

Fixed pawns can pose problems in the endgame, too. The outcome may depend on which king is more aggressively placed. In Diagram 85, White to play has a winning advantage.

85
White wins Black's fixed pawn by force

White to move invades with the king, going from c5 to d6. Black's king is then forced to move away from the e6-pawn and abandon it to White's king. With correct play thereafter, White will promote his e-pawn to a new queen.

The fixed pawns make it easy to plan and calculate around them because they cannot move. It's only when pawns can move that variations become complicated. Fixed pawns allow for more maneuvering and long-range planning—in other words, strategy.

In Diagram 86, there are only two pawns on the board and they are fixed. Since neither pawn can move, all the action is dependent on the moves of the kings. The static nature of the pawns makes for long-term planning and greater visualization.

86
Whoever moves first wins

White to play wins Black's g6-pawn by force. The key is to maneuver along the diagonal a2 to g8. With correct timing, White's king reaches d6 or e6, and from either square eventually occupies f6 to win the black pawn.

If Black moves first, however, the White pawn is won, and with proper play Black can promote his pawn. It's simply a matter of who moves first. Both fixed pawns are sitting ducks.

In both cases, the squares guarded by each side's fixed pawn—the strongpoints—prove critical. By controlling these squares, the pawn prevents the enemy king from mustering a workable defense.

IN REVIEW

Remember that fixed pawns generally allow for longer-range planning. When the fixed pawns occur in the center, they are important indicators of how each side should proceed.

In such cases, occupy your strongpoints—that is, the squares that your fixed pawn guards—and try to prevent the enemy from occupying his strongpoints.

Try to exchange your opponent's minor pieces that can reach the strongpoints. If possible, retain the option of guarding your opponent's strongpoints with pawns. This will effectively prevent the enemy's pieces from establishing themselves on those squares.

GOOD KNIGHT

♟ ♞ ♟

Bishops are usually better than knights because they have greater scope and can attack from farther away. knights have to be close to be effective. They usually need a pawn anchor to be secure, and they can't mark time as easily as bishops. They can't move and still guard the same squares, as a bishop can. But . . .

WHEN KNIGHTS ARE IN THE CATBIRD SEAT

Knights are better than bishops in three ways. Because they alternate colors with every move, they can guard squares of both colors. Because they can jump over other pieces, they can occupy otherwise inaccessible posts in the enemy camp. And they function well in closed positions, where bishops are severely hampered.

But bishops, even one that is not particularly strong, can offer much resistance. So if you have a good knight opposing a bad bishop, you must still play carefully to get the most out of the position.

The following example demonstrates some aspects of a knight's superiority. In Diagram 87, White's knight is significantly stronger than Black's bishop.

The pawns, except for White's doubled h-pawn at h2, cannot move. Black's pawns are fixed on the same color as his bishop, so the bishop's mobility is somewhat hampered. Black cannot afford to exchange the bishop for the knight, even though it would be normal procedure to get rid of a bad piece for a good one of equal value. The reason is that in the resulting king-and-pawn endgame, White's better-placed king would give him a winning advantage, especially since White has the only pawn moves. With extra pawn

87
White has a good knight

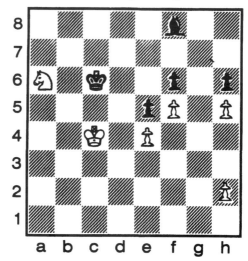

moves, White can gain a tempo (a unit of time based on the move, in which one tempo is equal to one move) if needed, assisting his king to get the upper hand.

With correct play, White's king and knight can make inroads, the knight anchoring eventually on d5 or e6. This would be an intolerable situation for Black.

Suppose White's knight checks on b4 to start. It would not be wise for Black to exchange down to an endgame, for White has those extra tempos. After Black moves his king to d6, White's knight invades on d5, assailing the f6-pawn. Black doesn't want to defend the pawn by moving his bishop to e7, for White could then trade minor pieces and win the king-and-pawn endgame. So Black defends the f6-pawn with the bishop from g7 (Diagram 88).

White could move his king to b5 right away, or he could maneuver his knight to g4 instead. From there the knight would look over both Black weaknesses at f6 and h6. So White continues by reposting his knight first to e3. Black's king returns to c6, and White follows by planting the knight on g4. After the Black king shifts back to d6, White's king invades on b5 (Diagram 89).

Let's say Black gives ground here, retreating his king to d7 (e7 is also possible). White's response is to move his king to c5. Black's

88
White has made inroads

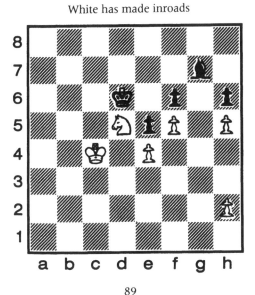

89
Black to move; White is closing in

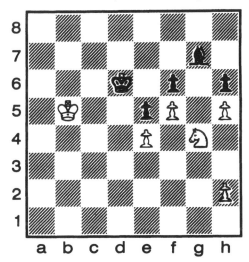

king opposes White's from c7. White's king sidles to d5, and
Black's king opposes again, shifting to d7 (Diagram 90).

For now, Black is holding off White's incursions. If White didn't

90
White to move; a tempo is needed

have a pawn at h2, he would not be able to make progress. But moving the h-pawn one square to h3 gains a tempo and forces Black to give ground. The Black bishop is an idle spectator in these proceedings, solely tied to defense.

After Black's king retreats to e7, White's king steps to c6. Black's bishop, free to move to f8 now that f6 is guarded by the king, does so. White now maneuvers the knight back to d5 by first moving it to e3. The bishop goes to g7, and the knight continues to d5, giving check. After Black's king retreats to e8, White's king invades to d6 (Diagram 91).

Black makes the only reasonable move, king to f7, and White's king pushes on to d7. Again Black can move his bishop to f8, since f6 is again protected by the king.

White's knight now begins its final maneuver, retreating to e3. Black tries to activate his bishop with a move to a3. White gains time by attacking it with his knight from c4. The bishop escapes to c1, and the knight checks on d6. After Black's king flees to g7, White's king reaches e6. Black adds protection to his f-pawn, moving his bishop to g5, but White wins the pawn anyway when the knight goes to e8, forking it and the king (Diagram 92).

91
White has gained significant ground

92
Black must lose the f-pawn and the game

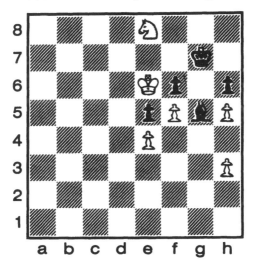

Black must abandon the f-pawn, which then falls to the combined attack of White's king and knight. The good knight has danced rings around the faltering bishop.

ADVICE

If you have a good knight against an inferior bishop, avoid trading these pieces. Keep the enemy bishop tied down to defending pawns and weak squares. Keep it blocked, and don't give it time to relocate. Use the knight's maneuverability to make inroads, especially in endgame positions where your king is free to assist.

But remember to save your pawn moves. If you squander them, you may not be able to gain a tempo when you need to. This is a significant disadvantage of the knight: it can't move and guard the same set of squares afterward. And it needs help from other pieces and pawns to maintain its position.

ISOLATED PAWN

An isolated pawn is one that cannot be protected by a friendly pawn. If attacked by the enemy, it must be defended by a piece. Pieces anchored to defense tend to be passive, and passive pieces can put you at a disadvantage.

Diagram 93 is an illustration of isolated white pawns. Black to move wins the g-pawn in three moves.

93
White's pawns are isolated

ATTACK THE ISOLATED PAWN

The chess adage "An isolated pawn spreads gloom" has more than a little truth to it. Your entire game may suffer because of the need to defend an isolated pawn.

In Diagram 94, White's rooks and bishop are tied down to the e-pawn's protection. Meanwhile, Black's rooks and bishop are all focused on that pawn.

94
The isolated e-pawn impairs White's game

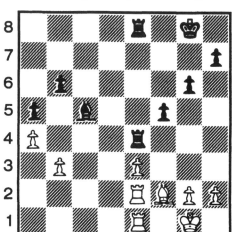

If it were Black's turn, he could win the e-pawn by attacking it again, advancing the f-pawn from f5 to f4. White's e-pawn would be assailed four times, and he would not have a fourth defender for it. White could not capture the f-pawn with the e3-pawn because it is pinned by Black's rooks. If White's e-pawn were to capture Black's f-pawn at f4, Black's rook on e4 would take White's rook on e2, and whether White's rook recaptured or not, Black would remain a rook ahead.

If it were White's turn, White could stop Black's threat to advance the f-pawn by moving his g-pawn from g2 to g3, guarding f4 a second time. Even so, White's position would remain feeble: 1) the light squares on the kingside would be weak; 2) the bishop at f2 would be locked in by its own pawns and practically unable to move; 3) the two rooks would be relegated to a purely defensive role on a closed file.

At best, White hopes Black will waste time, allowing White's king to assist, perhaps from f3. Once the e3-pawn has additional protection, White might be able to activate his other pieces. But Black keeps the upper hand, all because of the isolated pawn.

THE SQUARE IN FRONT

The square immediately in front of an isolated pawn is generally vulnerable to occupation by an enemy piece. If you're the one with the isolated pawn, this could have serious consequences for you; if your opponent has it, you can exploit the weakness to your advantage.

If the pawn were not isolated, a friendly pawn on an adjacent file might be able to move up and seize control of the square in question, preventing the enemy piece from occupying it. Or if an enemy piece were already occupying that square, a friendly neighboring pawn could drive the invader away.

Diagram 95 illustrates the weakness of the square in front of the isolated pawn.

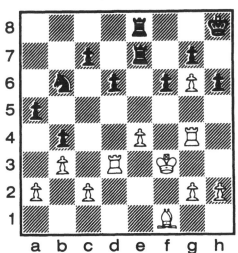

95
White cannot guard e5 with a pawn

White's e4-pawn is isolated. It cannot be protected by a friendly pawn. It is attacked twice, by Black's rooks at e7 and e8, the e8-Rook backing up the one at e7. White, meanwhile, is defending the e-pawn twice, with the king from f3 and the rook from g4.

The e5-square in front of the isolated pawn can't be guarded by a White pawn because there is no White pawn on an adjacent file. Black, on the other hand, solidly guards e5, with doubled rooks and two pawns, one at d6 and one at f6. White's e-pawn therefore cannot safely advance if it is attacked: It is a fixed target.

KNIGHTS IN FRONT OF THE PAWN

Each side has a minor piece: Black a knight at b6 and White a bishop at f1. White's bishop could be brought out to add defense to the e-pawn because both are on light squares. Even so, the bishop has little mobility because most of White's pawns, on light squares, obstruct the bishop's diagonal lines.

Although the light-square bishop can protect the isolated pawn, it has no effect on the dark e5-square in front of it. That central square makes a natural power base for Black's knight to occupy.

Black to move wins material by temporarily retreating the knight to d7. (You might say the knight is not retreating but advancing backward!) From d7, the knight is poised to take e5. White's two rooks and king are poorly positioned, and all three could be attacked by the Black knight on e5.

SAVE THE ROOK?

After the knight move to d7, White must lose the exchange, a rook for a knight. Even though Black's plan is obvious, White has no means to prevent its carrying out. If White moves the rook on d3 in an effort to save it, Black's knight goes to e5 with check and captures the g4-rook a move later.

If White tries to save the g4-rook instead, Black's knight still jumps to e5 with check, and one move later captures the d3-rook.

And if White moves his king from f3 to avoid the looming check, Black's knight leaps to e5 forking the two white rooks.

Here, the square in front of the isolated pawn, e5, is strong for Black and weak for White.

WEAK IN THE ENDGAME

An isolated pawn can be weak in the endgame too. In Diagram 96, Black's king can exploit the weak square, a3, in front of White's isolated pawn. This invasion enables Black to force a win.

96

Black's king heads for the weak square in front of the isolated pawn

Black to move invades a3 with the king. White's king must retreat to b1 to defend the isolated pawn. The black b-pawn then advances from b5 to b4, leaving White no choice—the king must be shifted to a1. Black further advances the b-pawn from b4 to b3. White's a-pawn then captures Black's b-pawn, and Black's a-pawn takes back on b3. (If White were to turn down the exchange, playing the king back to b1, Black's b-pawn would go to b2, forcing White's king out.)

After Black's a-pawn recaptures on b3, White's king moves to its only square, b1. Black then marches the b-pawn to b2, White's king comes up to c2, and Black's king advances to a2, insuring the promotion of the b-pawn to a new queen.

SADDLING THE PAWN

If you're saddled with an isolated pawn, try to exchange it for a useful, connected enemy pawn. Once it's traded, you'll never have to defend it again, and so it will cease to be a liability. See Diagram 97.

97
White can exchange his weak f-pawn for a strong
Black pawn

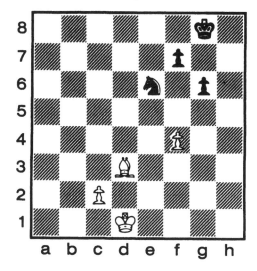

Black's knight eyes the capture of White's pawn at f4. White can't protect it, but he can advance it and force an exchange. When the White pawn is pushed to f5, it attacks Black's knight and g6-

pawn simultaneously. If Black's g6-pawn captures White's f5-pawn, the bishop recaptures on f5, and the White weakness has successfully been eliminated.

Should Black answer White's advance by moving his knight to f8 or f4 to defend the g-pawn, White simply captures on g6, and again, White has gotten rid of the isolated pawn problem.

THREATENING EXCHANGE

The threat to get rid of a weak isolated pawn by advancing and exchanging it is the reason the enemy tries to control the square immediately in front of the isolated pawn: to prevent just that threat.

But an isolated pawn isn't always a weakness—surely not if it can't be attacked or exploited. Sometimes it can even be wielded as an offensive weapon. It can be used as a battering ram to break apart the enemy's position. In Diagram 98, White sacrifices the isolated e-pawn to undermine Black's kingside fortress.

98
The isolated e-pawn becomes an attack weapon

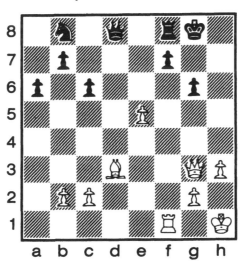

White breaks through and punctures Black's game by advancing the e-pawn to e6. If Black's f-pawn captures on e6, White's queen crashes through on g6, mating on h7 one move later.

OTHER STRATEGIES

How can Black defend if he doesn't want to capture White's e-pawn once it reaches e6? If he adds protection to the f-pawn, perhaps by moving the queen to e7, White captures Black's f-pawn with check, Black's rook recaptures on f7, and White's queen then perforates Black's thin veil by capturing the g6-pawn with check (Diagram 99). No matter how Black replies, something is lost.

99
White wins no matter how Black gets out of check

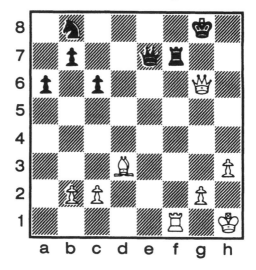

If Black gets out of check by interposing the rook on g7, White's bishop checks at c4, forcing Black's king to h8. White's queen then checks at h6, forcing Black's rook to block at h7. White's rook now checks at f8, Black's queen must capture the rook, and White's queen retakes on f8, giving mate.

In the Diagram, if Black moves his king to f8, White's rook captures Black's on f7 (White also gains by checking on h6), Black's queen takes back, and White's queen slides to d6, forking Black's king and knight.

Finally, if Black moves the king to the h8-corner right away, White simply takes the f7-rook for nothing.

The advance of the isolated e-pawn crushed Black's defenses.

THE PAWN AS AN ANCHOR

Sometimes an isolated pawn has value if it is far advanced and is used to anchor a friendly piece in the heart of the enemy camp, as in Diagram 100.

100
The isolated pawn will anchor the knight

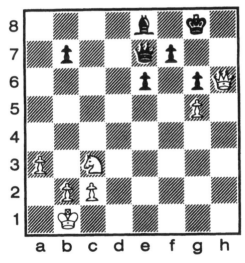

White wins by moving the c3-knight to e4, threatening a deadly check at f6. To stop mate Black will have to surrender his queen for the knight when it comes to f6.

Other defenses fail. For example, if Black answers White's knight-move to e4 by moving the f7 pawn to f5 (to create an escape square for the king), White's knight checks on f6 anyway, Black's king goes to f7, and White's queen parachutes in on h7 with check. Black's king retreats to f8, and White's queen puts the lid on the coffin at g8 (Diagram 101).

101
Black is mated

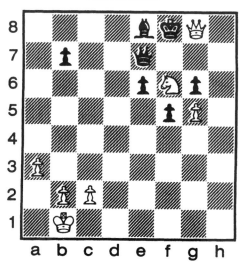

102
White's isolated pawn is passed and will promote

CONVERTING THE PAWN

Occasionally, an isolated pawn can be converted into a passed pawn; that is, a pawn that can't be stopped from advancing by an enemy pawn because there is no enemy pawn on the same file and no enemy pawn that guards any squares in its path.

The pawn, in a sense, has "passed" all enemy pawns. Such a pawn may be able to advance to become a new queen if enemy pieces cannot stop its march.

Diagram 102 shows an isolated pawn that is a passed pawn.

White's a-pawn will become a new queen. It doesn't matter who goes first—White promotes by force.

LURING OFF THE BLOCKERS

To convert an isolated pawn into a passed pawn, the enemy pawn or pawns that block or guard its path must be lured away. Diagram 103 offers a conclusive example.

103
White transforms the b-pawn into a passed pawn

White to move wins by advancing the d-pawn to d6, threatening to capture Black's c-pawn. If Black takes White's d-pawn, his c-pawn is diverted from the c-file, and White's b-pawn then moves through unstoppably to b8.

If Black instead moves his c-pawn to either c6 or c5, again White's b-pawn skates through unmolested. A new White queen will result, for Black's king is too far away to catch the b-pawn.

TENDING TO WEAKNESS

In most cases, isolated pawns tend to be weak. (The isolated queen-pawn is a special case and is discussed under its own heading.) If attacked, isolated pawns must be guarded by pieces, which reduces their activity. Additionally, the square immediately in front of an isolated pawn is vulnerable because it cannot be guarded by a friendly pawn.

If you are attacking an isolated pawn, make sure you are in secure control of the square in front of it to prevent your target from moving away. Once its advance is prevented, pile up on it with as many pieces as are available.

If possible, use the square in front of it as a base to raid the enemy position. Try to eliminate any pieces that can be called up for defense duty.

Try to exchange your isolated pawn for a healthy pawn by advancing it. Failing that, try to develop counterplay elsewhere to divert your opponent from attacking the pawn effectively.

CONSIDER SACRIFICE

If you as the attacker are saddled with an isolated pawn, consider sacrificing it to break up your opponent's defenses. Avoid exchanges that result in a premature endgame in which you have no counterplay and cannot exchange off your isolated weakness.

If your isolated pawn is far advanced, it will probably be difficult to defend. Sometimes, however, such a pawn can be used to anchor one of your pieces (especially a knight) deep in the enemy's position.

More generally: don't let your isolated pawn spoil your game. If it hampers you, get rid of it or make it work for you. Do what the position requires. Never give your opponent a breather.

ISOLATED
D-PAWN

An isolated d-pawn is a pawn on the d-file that has no pawns to support it on either the c-file or the e-file. It is also known as the isolated queen-pawn because it's on the file that the two queens occupy in the opening.

Since the isolated d-pawn can't be protected by a friendly pawn if attacked, it must be defended by pieces. It is therefore a likely target of your opponent's attack.

An isolated d-pawn can be situated anywhere along the d-file, from d2 to d7, but, practically speaking, the discussion of the isolated d-pawn usually focuses on the two center squares, d4 and d5. These two squares are where isolated d-pawns are most often found in a whole complex of frequently played openings.

THE PATTERNS OF ISOLATION

Diagrams 104 and 105 are mirror images of the basic pawn skeletons in which either White or Black has an isolated d-pawn.

In both diagrams, the c-file is completely open to both Black and White. This type of position, which we'll call Pattern A, often arises when White opens with a double advance of the d-pawn.

Diagrams 106 and 107 are also mirror images of each other. Here the common open file is the e-file. We'll call this type of position Pattern B.

These types of positions arise most often when White opens the game by pushing the e-pawn two squares.

104
White has an isolated d-pawn (Pattern A)

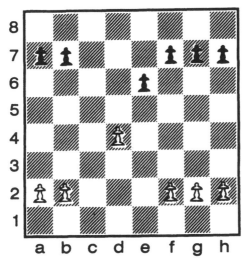

105
Black has an isolated d-pawn (Pattern A)

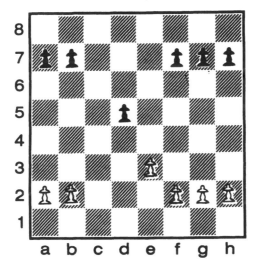

106
White has an isolated d-pawn (Pattern B)

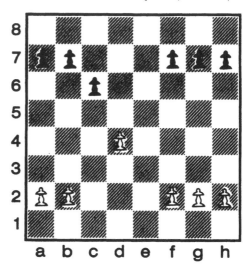

107
Black has an isolated d-pawn (Pattern B)

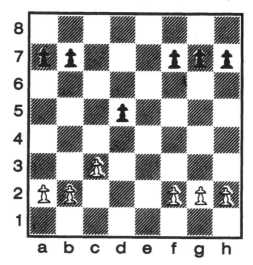

ORIGINS OF ISOLATED D-PAWNS

In the opening, the back-rank forces must be mobilized as quickly as possible. This process is called development. One by one, the officers are brought into position from their home squares to effective battle stations. To be effective, these developing pieces must come in contact with or have some influence on at least one of the central squares—d4, e4, d5, or e5.

A struggle for control of the center ensues. The e- and d-pawns play particularly important roles in the development process. The center pawn advances open lines of development for the bishops while staking out territory in the board's center.

But the d- and e-pawns are not the only ones fighting for the center. The c-pawns, or the queen-bishop-pawns, frequently play an active part in the central struggle. The c-pawn can be used offensively, to assail the enemy d-pawn, or defensively, to support its friendly neighboring d-pawn. It is when the c-pawn is called into action that isolated d-pawn structures are created.

THE AGGRESSIVE D-PAWN

Diagram 108 is a snapshot from an opening in progress. White began by playing the d-pawn up two squares, from d2 to d4, and the position shown comes from a variation of the Queen's Gambit Declined.

In this position, both players are using their c-pawns aggressively: The White c-pawn attacks Black d-pawn; the Black c-pawn pressures the White d-pawn. Depending on which pawn exchanges take place, either side—or both—could wind up with an isolated d-pawn.

White to play in this position can initiate a series of exchanges resulting in Black having an isolated d-pawn. For example, he can trade the d-pawn for the Black c5-pawn, and after Black recap-

108
A position from the Queen's Gambit Declined

tures on c5 with his f8-bishop, White captures the d5-pawn with his c4-pawn. After Black takes back on d5 with his e-pawn we get the position of Diagram 109.

109
Black has an isolated d-pawn

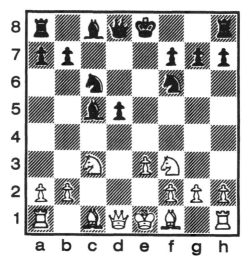

Going back to Diagram 108, if White elects to continue development by playing his f1-bishop to d3, it is he who could end up with the isolated d-pawn. Black takes the pawn at c4 with the d5-pawn. White naturally recaptures at c4 with the d3-bishop, Black snips off the d4-pawn with his c5-pawn, and White restores material equality by recapturing on d4 with his e3-pawn. Diagram 110 shows the resulting position.

110
White has an isolated d-pawn

PROTECTIONIST ISOLATION

In Diagram 108, which began as a queen-pawn opening, the c-pawns were used as shock troops to assault the enemy d-pawns. In king-pawn openings, in which White brings out the e-pawn two squares, the c-pawn often plays a helping role by supporting the d-pawn's advance to the d4 center square.

Diagram 111 shows a typical case from the Giuoco Piano, Greco Variation.

The White c3-pawn's role is clearly one of protection, enabling the White d-pawn to advance to d4, where it attacks both the Black c5-bishop and the e5-pawn.

111
The Greco Variation

112
White is in check

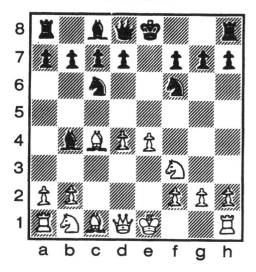

A retreat by Black's bishop to d6 would now be very poor, since it would block the advance of the d7-pawn and severely constrict Black's position. Black must therefore capture the White d4-pawn with the e5-pawn, and White follows with the planned recapture by the c3-pawn to d4. Black saves the attacked c5-bishop without loss of time by checking the White king at b4—Diagram 112.

BREAKING UP THE CENTER

White interposes the queen-bishop at d2, Black captures the bishop with check, and White retakes with the b1-knight coming to d2. Now Black breaks up the strong White pawn center with the double advance of the d-pawn, producing the position of Diagram 113.

113
The White pawn center is challenged

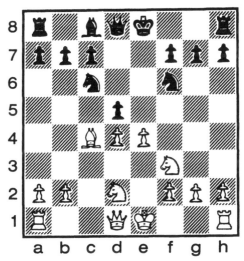

A CHARACTERISTIC PATTERN

White saves the attacked bishop by capturing the Black d5-pawn with his e4-pawn, and Black recaptures the pawn with his knight on f6, backed up by his queen on d8. The resulting position, Diagram 114, is an isolated d-pawn structure of the Pattern B type (also see Diagram 106).

114
A Pattern B position

COMPARING POSITIONS

In comparing the pawn structure of Diagram 114 with that of Diagram 106, you will find only one minor difference. In Diagram 106 Black's c-pawn is on c6, while in Diagram 114 it is still on c7. Nevertheless, both are clearly Pattern B positions because the isolated d-pawn is flanked by a vacant e-file (and in the position of Diagram 114 the c-pawn will soon be played to c6 anyway).

White to play in Diagram 114 moves his queen to b3, adding a second attack to Black's d5-knight. Since the knight is guarded only by the d8-queen, Black swings the c6 knight to e7 for additional support.

Both White and Black castle kingside. White now plays the newly developed f1-rook to e1, the open king-file. Here Black takes a moment to safeguard the strong d5-knight by playing the c7-pawn up one square to c6. The position of Diagram 115 is now unmistakably a classic Pattern B.

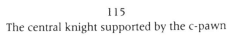

115
The central knight supported by the c-pawn

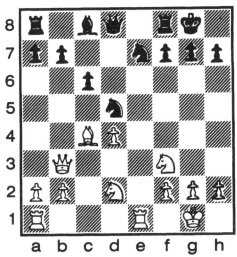

WHY NO ISOLATED E-PAWN

It's easy to create an isolated d-pawn when both center pawns as well as the c-pawn participate to control the center squares. In a great many openings, these three pawns are logically connected with the struggle for domination of the center. Pawn trades take place naturally, the c- and e-pawns are exchanged, and one side or the other ends up with an isolated d-pawn.

For an isolated e-pawn to appear on the board, its neighboring d- and f-pawns must obviously disappear, leaving one side or the other with only an e-pawn. But although it's easy enough to rid yourself of a d-pawn—all you have to do is advance both center pawns two squares, and an exchange of pawns on d5 or d4 is almost inevitable—the f-pawn is another matter.

THE F-PAWN'S FUNCTION

As a rule, f-pawns do not take part in the struggle for the center. Unlike the c-pawn, the f-pawn must safeguard the king.

116
The castled king

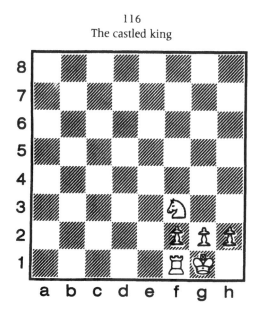

Diagram 116 shows a typical castled position that arises naturally in many different openings. Experienced players protect the king by castling, most often on the kingside.

THE KINGSIDE MAY BE SAFER

Kings are generally safer on the kingside than on the queenside. Also, there are fewer pieces to get out of the way before castling can take place—only two on the kingside but three on the queenside.

The three kingside pawns, the f-pawn, g-pawn, and h-pawn, stand on their original squares. With the protecting knight on f3 (f6 for Black), this forms the strongest possible defense of the castled position. The pawns form a protective cocoon around the king, guarding it from enemy attack. Pawns are strongest defensively when standing on their home squares. In Diagram 116, White should normally be very reluctant to move any of the three pawns guarding the king. And the knight guards key squares that the opponent needs for attack. The three pawns and the knight can't leave their posts without endangering the castled position.

That's why e-pawns rarely become isolated. The f-pawn usually stays back to preserve the safety of the king. If it doesn't advance, it can't be traded off, and if it isn't traded, there's no isolated e-pawn.

ISOLATED D-PAWN: ADVANCING IT

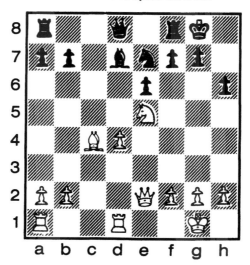

So far, we've been discussing the isolated d-pawn as a static entity. The advance of the d-pawn can have the effect of energizing the position and opening attack lines for first rank pieces.

In Diagram 117, White's rook is facing the black queen on d8, a fact that could spell trouble for Black if the d-file is opened. So White opens it by advancing the d-pawn, threatening mayhem at e6. This attack leads to a series of exchanges on the d5-square.

117
White moves and opens the d-file

First, Black takes the d5-pawn with the e-pawn, and White recaptures at d5 with his c4-bishop. Now Black takes the d5-bishop with the knight, and White's rook recaptures (Diagram 118).

THE KING IS DEAD

118
Black moves; the pinned bishop is lost

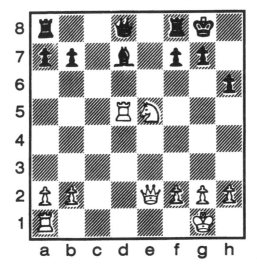

The d-file is completely open and the d7-bishop is now pinned by the rook to the Black queen. Since the bishop is doubly attacked (by the rook and the knight), Black must lose at least a piece, and this will cost him the game.

OPENING LINES

In Diagram 119, Black has a solid game and is leading in development, but White has some advantages, too. His e1-rook is well placed, and his queen and bishop are aligned dangerously against the h7-square, which for the moment is protected by the Black knight on f6.

119
White plays and opens the e-file

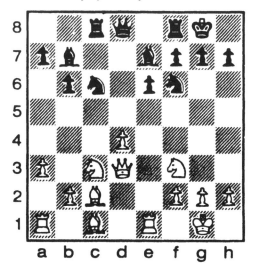

120
White moves and exploits the e-file

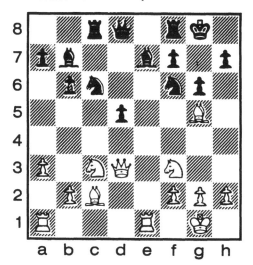

White converts potential to reality by advancing the d-pawn to d5. When Black takes on d5 with the e6-pawn, White slides the c1-bishop to g5, threatening to take the black f6-knight and then mate on h7 with the queen. Black blocks this threat by bringing the g-pawn to g6 (Diagram 120).

White directs his energy at the f6-knight, whose support was weakened by the Black g-pawn advance. White now weakens its support still further by eliminating the e7-bishop with an exchange sacrifice: e1-rook takes e7-bishop.

GAINING A KNIGHT

This sacrifice is temporary, and in fact it's not really a sacrifice at all, for White eventually wins material. When Black takes the rook with the queen, White's c3-knight captures Black's d5-pawn (Diagram 121).

121
White gains the f6-knight

Black's f6-knight is still pinned by White's g5-bishop. White's d5-knight, moreover, attacks both Black's queen and Black's f6-knight. At the least, White will gain the material advantage of two minor pieces for a rook.

REALITY

Our final example of an advancing d-pawn is a complex position from the opening phase of an actual game. Development is incomplete, and neither player has castled (Diagram 122).

122
White can advance the d-pawn

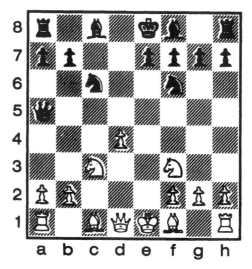

It's early in the game. The Black e-pawn hasn't yet advanced to e6, and this makes the forward march of White's d-pawn to d5 inviting, especially because it gains time, forcing Black's attacked c6-knight to move to the wing.

Nevertheless, the push of the d4-pawn to d5 must not be made automatically. Advance a pawn into enemy territory only when you are sure you can defend it. Here the d5-thrust is quite strong.

After Black relocates the c6-knight to b4, Black has three units attacking d5 and White has but two defending it (Diagram 123).

White has several possible ways to save the d-pawn. Two of these require the light-square bishop to be moved, which also prepares for kingside castling. The bishop can go to b5, giving check to Black's king, or to c4, guarding the d5-pawn.

123
The advanced d-pawn is under fire

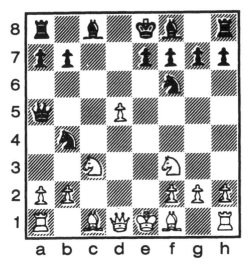

White decides on a third possibility, moving an entirely different piece and attacking the b4-knight: he plays his a-pawn to a3 (Diagram 124).

124
White attacks the b4-knight

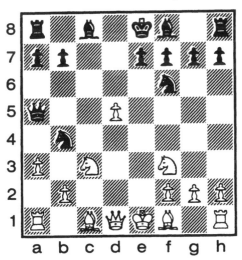

SNIPING AWAY

White's last two moves were consistent. First the d-pawn attacked Black's c6-knight, and now the a-pawn snipes at it again. But these moves raise a few questions.

White's last move doesn't contribute to development, nor does it help protect the d5-pawn. Besides, can White actually carry out his threat to capture Black's b4-knight? If he takes the knight with the a-pawn, Black's queen can take White's a1-rook.

The position requires deep analysis.

How should Black respond to White's last move? The most brutal response would be to capture the d5-pawn with the b4-knight (Diagram 125).

125
Black takes the bait

Black calculated that the three attackers (the a5-queen, b4-knight, and f6-knight) would overwhelm White's two defenders (the d1-queen and the c3-knight). Based solely on the ratio of attackers to defenders, this was correct. But Black considered only direct defenses. White actually has an indirect defense of d5. The d-pawn was merely the bait in a clever trap.

White now plays his bishop from f1 to b5, checking Black's king. Black must block the check at d7 with the c8-bishop. White's b5-Bishop then captures Black's on d7, and Black's king must retake on d7, bringing the king onto the same file as White's queen (Diagram 126).

126
Black's d5-knight is lost

The first reason for the advance of White's a-pawn is now revealed: The pawn on a3 supports the b-pawn's advance to b4, attacking Black's queen on a5. When the queen moves to a safe square, it will no longer be protecting the d5-knight, which White could then capture, winning material.

Note the importance of luring Black's king to the d-file. If the king were still on e8, the d5-knight could capture the b4-pawn, but with the king on d7 the d5-knight is pinned by White's queen at d1.

DEVELOPING THE BISHOP

We have analyzed one of the possibilities in Diagram 124, Black capturing the d5-pawn with the b4-knight, which resulted in a loss for Black.

Now let's see what happens if Black doesn't take White's d5-pawn, but develops his c8-bishop to f5 instead (Diagram 127).

127
Black develops the bishop with a threat

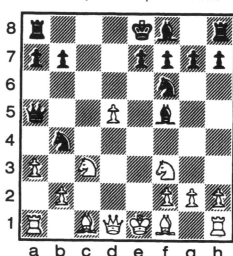

With Black's bishop at f5, White's c2-square is menaced by both that bishop and Black's b4-knight. If the knight can go to c2, it will fork White's king and a1-rook.

White might consider several possibilities, including giving check at b5 with the light-squared bishop, or stationing the f3-knight at d4 to defend c2. But White, knowing what lies ahead, takes Black's b4-knight, getting rid of the attack on his c2. Black's queen then captures White's a1-rook, and White follows with the repositioning of the f3-knight to d4 (Diagram 128).

When an isolated d-pawn advances, the square it vacates be-

128
Black's queen is threatened

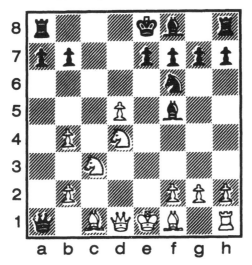

comes available to friendly pieces. White's f3-knight can make use of the vacated d4 as a pivot, attacking in two directions at once. It threatens to capture the f5-bishop and threatens also to jump back to b3, trapping Black's hapless queen on a1.

Black has only one satisfactory answer: to invade with the f6-knight to e4, hoping to capture White's c3-knight and provide an escape for the queen at a1.

White, realizing an exchange is inevitable, takes Black's e4-knight with the c3-knight, and Black's f5-bishop recaptures on e4. Next comes a check at b5 by White's king-bishop. Black's king must go to d8 (Diagram 129).

MONARCH UNDER SIEGE

White's advancing d-pawn set off a chain reaction. Initially, White's attention was directed against Black's queen-knight. The advance d4 to d5 menaced it, as did the nudge a2 to a3. The knight later fell to a pawn capture.

129
Black's king is under fire

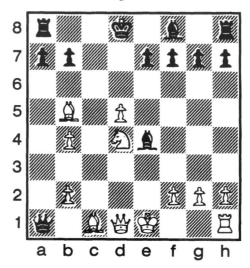

130
White discovers a shot

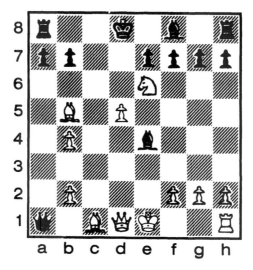

Then Black's queen came under fire. Poorly positioned at a1, where it was out of action and lacked mobility, the queen was in danger of being trapped. Black managed to counter by invading with the f6-knight to e4, but now, after the exchange of minor pieces, Black's king, unable to castle, has come under heavy fire. No immediate defenders are available and the harried king must fend for itself.

In the position of Diagram 129, White turns up the heat with a spectacular move. He plays the d4-knight to e6, checking Black's king. This move deserves its own picture (Diagram 130).

Black can't afford to take the e6-knight. If the f7-pawn captures on e6, then White recaptures on e6 with the d5-pawn, unveiling a discovered check from White's queen on d1.

How is Black's king going to get out of this discovered check? If it goes to c8, White checkmates in two moves: the queen moves to d7 and on the next move to d8.

If Black moves the king to c7, another discovered attack ensues, but this time directed against Black's queen: White's c1-bishop moves to f4, checking Black's king, and on the next move White's queen captures Black's.

This analysis shows the magnificent coordination between the advancing d-pawn and its rear guard. White's knight made excellent use of d4, and White's d1-queen was ready for action.

PLAYING THE GAME

Returning to the game, Black realizes that in Diagram 130 the knight on e6 can't safely be captured. So Black must move his king to c8. White then follows with a devastating quiet move and simply castles (Diagram 131).

White needed to call up the reserves, so he got the king tucked away and mobilized the king-rook. This luxury, the ability to castle, was White's alone: Black never had time to castle.

131
Black's move: the calm before the storm

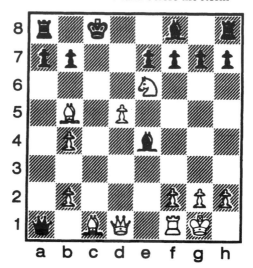

132
White to play: Black's queen tries a comeback

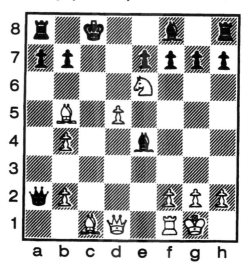

QUEEN ON THE MOVE

White's castling move re-energizes the entire game, coordinating pieces beautifully. Before castling, White's queen was tied to protecting the c1-bishop. But now the f1-rook defends c1, and suddenly the White queen is free to move. The newly liberated queen might even try to occupy d4, previously occupied by the isolated d-pawn, a good transfer square.

Black isn't in check, and has a momentary respite. How should the defense be organized? Capturing the e6-knight remains out of the question because when the d-file is opened the White queen penetrates with fatal effect.

Counterattacking the b5-bishop by moving the a7-pawn to a6 doesn't work: White just ignores the attack and centralizes thematically on the d4-square with the queen. White would then have a winning attack, especially the threat of queen to c5 followed by mate.

In the actual game, Black opted to move the queen to a2, with the idea of capturing the d5-pawn and bringing the queen back into action (Diagram 132).

White develops the bishop from c1 to f4, looking toward Black's king. With c1 now vacant, White's queen prepares to put it to use: a crushing check!

Clearly, Black doesn't have time to take the d-pawn. Instead, Black's queen captures the b2-pawn, and after White's queen checks at c1, Black's queen blocks at c2 (Black's queen can't take White's, because White's rook recaptures with check, and it's mate next move). See Diagram 133.

PAYING THE PIPER

Black has only two pieces in the field—a queen and bishop—and they can't possibly cope with a fully organized force. First White's queen captures Black's queen, giving check. Black's bishop takes back on c2. Then White follows with a cruncher: the

133
White to play: Black makes a last stand

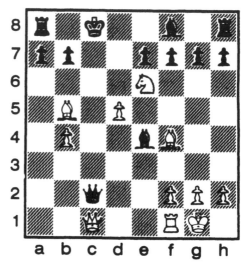

134
White moves in for the kill

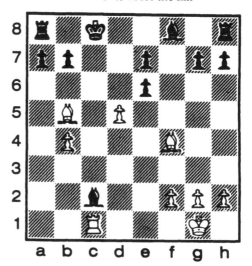

f1-rook slides over to c1, pinning the bishop at c2 and threatening instant mate.

Black has no choice. He must take the knight at e6 to give his king an escape square at d8 (Diagram 134).

The Black king stands alone against three pieces and can't muster a defense. White dispatches Black's king quickly and mercifully.

First he takes the c2-bishop with the rook, giving check. Black gets out of check by moving the king to d8. Then the f4-bishop intrudes to c7, checking Black's king again and forcing it back to c8. Appropriately, the final move of the game belongs to White's d-pawn: It captures on e6 (Diagram 135).

135
The final position: Black gives up

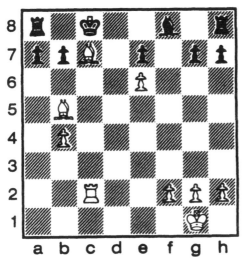

Black resigns because mate next move is unavoidable. White's b5-bishop goes to d7. If Black tries to create an escape square by moving the b-pawn to b6, White's bishop delivers mate anyway, at a6.

The complex nature of isolated d-pawn positions suggested a thorough analysis of a real chess game. We have seen how an advancing isolated d-pawn can be quite powerful. Even at the very end, this pawn served a valuable function. Having become, technically, an e-pawn, it supports the bishop check at d7.

ADVICE

If you have an isolated d-pawn, try to keep your pieces active. Look to establishing knight outposts on the central squares. Be alert, moreover, to advancement opportunities for the isolated d-pawn.

But in pushing the isolated d-pawn, understand the risks. Without the right back-up, the d-pawn could fall victim to the closeness of the enemy attackers. Balance this risk against the obvious advantages of such an advance. The rooks get open lines behind the advanced d-pawn. The central square d4 is available to be occupied, especially by a knight. And, if the situation calls for aggressive, sacrificial play, be prepared to enter upon that path. It may be the only way to realize your advantage or avoid defeat.

Naturally, great demands are placed on the player who accepts an isolated d-pawn. You must play with exceptional energy, never allowing your attention to wander. You must see the entire board, not just a specific sector. Pieces may shift into action across the center, from one side of the board to the other, at a move's notice.

Calculation of possible variations is a necessity. Your analysis must be precise and penetrating. In short, if you want to improve your game, try to play openings that generate isolated d-pawns. Be willing to take either side; to play with the isolated d-pawn and to play against it. All aspects of your play will improve.

ISOLATED D-PAWN: DRAWBACKS

♟ ♞ ♟

After all is said and done, the isolated d-pawn is still an isolated pawn, sharing the same inherent weaknesses as all other isolated pawns. These weaknesses are twofold:

First, an attacked isolated d-pawn must be defended by friendly pieces because there are simply no friendly pawns to do the job. This ties the pieces down, taking them out of active play. Due to their loss of mobility, the pieces guarding an isolated pawn may themselves well become targets of enemy attack.

Second, the square immediately in front of the isolated d-pawn is weak. Commonly called the blockade square, it can easily be co-opted by enemy pieces. Since no c- or e-pawn can dislodge the enemy piece from this square, a blockading piece entrenched there can immobilize the isolated d-pawn while constantly threatening to invade the surrounding terrain.

BLOCKADING THE ISOLATED D-PAWN

Diagram 136 shows a typical situation, with Black laying siege to the d4 isolated pawn. Black's rook has an excellent post on the d5 blockade square, preventing any movement by White's d4-pawn and fixing it for attack.

Black's rook and knight continuously threaten to capture the isolated d-pawn, which means that the White knight and rook must stay at their posts to protect it.

136
Frontal attack: Black to move

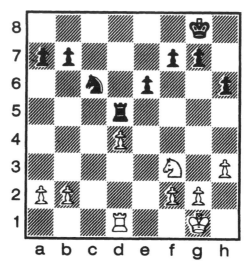

A BALANCING ACT

Attack and defense are in balance. Black has two attackers trained on the d4-pawn; White has two defenders. As often happens, however, the pieces defending the isolated d-pawn are not well placed, especially the rook, which is unprotected.

Black to move in Diagram 136 introduces a third attacker against the d4-pawn by advancing the e-pawn to e5. There is no third defender for White. Nor can White capture the newly advanced e-pawn: the d4-pawn is pinned because the White rook is not protected. If White now took the black e-pawn with the d-pawn, Black would simply take the White rook for nothing. Nor can White take e5 with the knight. Black would take the White knight at e5 with his knight, and again, the d4-pawn could not take back without losing the undefended d1-rook.

White has no way to defend the isolated d4-pawn; Black is assaulting it too many times. White has no choice but to allow Black to confiscate the pawn on the next move, undoubtedly with the e-pawn.

PINNING THE PAWN

Diagram 137 shows another pin against the isolated d-pawn. Here, Black takes advantage of the undefended White b2-bishop. Black has occupied the d5-square, and it's the king that's doing the blockading.

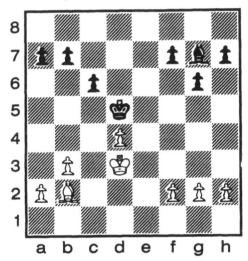

137
Diagonal attack: Black to move

Black's key move is the advance of the c-pawn to c5, assaulting the d4-pawn a third time: it is already attacked by the king and the bishop. White can only muster two defenders: the king and the bishop on b2.

The d4-pawn is pinned along the dark-square diagonal by the black g7-bishop. Should White make the mistake of capturing the c5-pawn with his d4-pawn, he would lose the bishop. Again, White is outgunned on the d4-square, and the isolated d-pawn must fall to Black's combined attack.

ENDGAME FLAVOR

Both Diagrams 136 and 137 have a pronounced endgame flavor. This is not accidental. As pieces are traded off and the position stripped down to its bare essentials, the isolated d-pawn's vulnerability becomes more and more evident. At the same time, with each exchange of pieces, the endgame draws nearer and the significance of the blockading squares increases in importance.

ADVICE

When playing *against* an isolated d-pawn, try to trade pieces so as to reach a favorable endgame. When playing *with* an isolated d-pawn, avoid indiscriminate piece exchanges. Try instead to keep pieces on the board and stay out of the endgame.

COMES THE END

In Diagram 138, each side has three pieces, including queens, on the board. Black, understanding that the isolated d-pawn weakness is best exploited in the endgame, quickly seizes the opportunity to trade queens. He takes White's queen at e1 and announces check to the enemy king. White must recapture with the rook, and Black then exchanges the a4-pawn for the White b3-pawn. White takes back at b3 with the a2-pawn (see Diagram 139).

PASSIVE AGGRESSIVE

Black has accomplished a great deal in only two moves. The elimination of the queens has removed any attacking potential for White. With queens on the board, White could hope to create some complications. But now White is reduced to passive defense.

138
Black to move: transition to the endgame

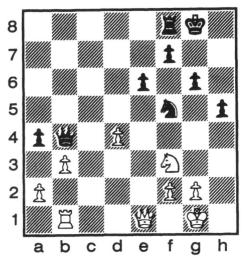

139
Black to move: aggressive rook vs. passive rook

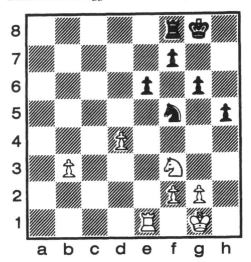

The rook, forced to recapture on e1, ends up on a feeble square. The exchange of Black's a-pawn for White's has also helped Black's game. White is now saddled with two weak, isolated pawns at d4 and b3.

DANCING AT TWO WEDDINGS

Black now activates his rook by bringing it to b8, the open b-file, attacking the undefended b3-pawn. White must defend it, and shifts his rook to b1. Now Black closes in, playing the rook to b4, initiating a horizontal attack on the isolated d4-pawn.

White can't defend both weak pawns. If he moves his rook to d1, Black rakes in the undefended b3-pawn with his rook. If White leaves the rook on the b-file, Black captures the d4-pawn with his knight. Either way, Black wins an important pawn.

A FULL STRENGTH ROOK

The play from Diagram 139 highlights an important difference in the value of the two rooks. A rook operating at full strength is normally worth the equivalent of five pawns (or "points"). In Diagram 139, it is only the Black rook that is pulling its true weight, seizing the open b-file and attacking the White pawn weaknesses at b3 and d4. The White rook, playing a defensive role, is working at only a fraction of its potential. This isn't a five-point rook.

Rooks, then, are much better pieces when they are on the attack. They are active and enjoy full mobility. They are full-value pieces. Rooks on defense are cumbersome and devalued; a rook's powers are diluted by defensive chores.

When playing against an isolated d-pawn, aim for a rook ending with active rooks. Seize open files; attack enemy weaknesses; try to keep your opponent's rook on the defense.

Conversely, when you have the isolated d-pawn, use your minor pieces to guard the pawn. This relieves your rook for active duty on open files, where it does its best work. Don't bog down your rook with passive, defensive drudgery.

ATTACKING TWICE

In Diagrams 138 and 139, the pieces guarding the isolated d4-pawn were undefended and vulnerable to a pinning tactic. Diagram 140 shows another technical device Black can use to exploit the isolated d-pawn's weakness: the double attack.

140
Black to move: double attack

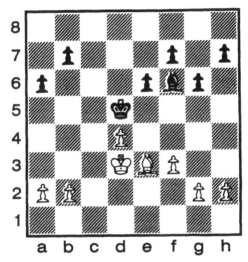

Black moves the king-pawn one square to e5, adding a third attacking unit against the d4-pawn. White must exchange the d4-pawn for the e5-pawn since the d4-pawn can't be defended a third time. But the capture on e5 allows Black to recapture with the bishop, which now simultaneously attacks two undefended White pawns, at b2 and h2. White can't save both, so he must lose a pawn to Black's double attack.

In this example, the d4 pawn was used as a lever to pry open White's position to Black's advantage.

SOFTENING UP THE TARGET

141
Removing the defender

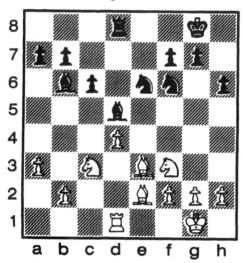

In Diagram 141, the White d4-pawn is defended three times: by the f3-knight, the e3-bishop, and the d1-rook. Black has three attacking units in place. Two of them, the b6-bishop and the e6-knight, have the d4-pawn directly in their sights; the third, the d8-rook, eyes the d4-pawn indirectly down the d-file, behind the Black d5-bishop.

The pieces defending the isolated d-pawn are immobile and themselves targets of attack.

THE ROOK'S FULL POWER

Black to play in Diagram 141 captures the defending f3-knight with the d5-bishop, removing one of the d4-pawn's defenders and unleashing the d8-rook's full power. White can't ignore the capture at f3, and retakes the Black bishop with his bishop at e2.

Now Black has numerical superiority directed against the d4-pawn with three attackers and only two defenders. Black can safely capture the pawn with the e6-knight, coming out a full pawn ahead.

Black's play was directed toward winning the isolated queen-pawn by removing one of its defenders, the f3-knight. In order to arrive at this position, Black had to insure control of the d5 blockade square. Control and occupation of the blockade square fixed the isolated d-pawn as a target and guaranteed that it couldn't advance. Black occupied the blockade square with a bishop while the f6-knight, the d8-rook, and the c6-pawn were all in contact with the vital d5 blockade point.

HOLDING THE BLOCKADE

142
Black to move: blockade square as an invasion point

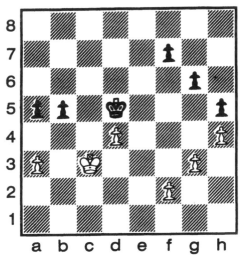

Diagram 142 is a pure king-and-pawn endgame, with Black's king already stationed on the important d5 blockade square, where it not only attacks the d-pawn but also threatens an invasion into

White's position from d5. If Black can successfully penetrate via the e4-square, White's entire kingside will be undefendable and his kingside pawns will be lost.

The Black king's immediate entry is impossible, however. White would reply by advancing the f2-pawn one square, giving check. Black would not be able to capture White's undefended f3-pawn because White's passed d-pawn would advance unhindered and become a new queen. Black's king wouldn't be able to get back in time to stop it. So, after White played the pawn to f3, Black would have to retreat to the d5 blockade square. That would still be favorable for Black, but there is something much better in the offing.

THE INVASION PROCEEDS

In Diagram 142, Black advances his b5-pawn to b4, giving check. White takes the pawn with his a3-pawn, and Black recaptures with his a5-pawn, again giving check. White now may as well take Black's undefended b-pawn—if he doesn't, it will simply advance and force him to take it.

143
Black to play: d4 falls and the invasion proceeds

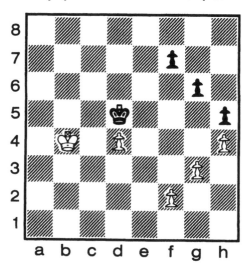

This is the position Black envisaged when advancing the b5-pawn. The White king is drawn away from the isolated d4-pawn's defense, leaving it open to capture by Black's king at d5. And after he takes it, White's kingside pawns are wide open. White's king is too far away from the action to stop Black from getting in among the kingside pawns and gobbling them up one by one.

THE BLACK KNIGHT INVADES

Diagrams 142 and 143 show how, in the endgame, the d5 blockade square can be a staging ground for invading enemy territory by the pieces occupying that square. Diagram 144 is a middlegame invasion position and the interloper is the Black knight.

144
The knight invades

Diagram 144 shows Black firmly established on the d5 blockading square, occupying it with a knight. The blockading knight is supported three times, by the f6-knight, the b7-queen, and the e6-pawn.

The knight is an ideal blockader. Its special ability to leap over intervening pieces and squares mean that even while blockading, its mobility and influence aren't reduced. Moreover, a knight is optimally placed in the board's center, where it can also attack, threaten, and support. A knight stationed on the central blockading square d5 is magnificently placed.

Black to play in Diagram 144 invades the White position by transferring the d5-knight to f4, which unleashes the powerful b7-queen. The knight and queen combine to threaten checkmate on g2. Notice, too, that the f4-knight threatens to win the White queen. Faced with two powerful threats, one to the king and the other to the queen, White has only one reply—the queen must go to f3. Any other move by the White queen would be disastrous. Moving it to h3 simply loses it to a knight capture. Playing it to g3 allows a crushing knight fork, knight to e2 check, again winning the White queen.

MATERIAL WILL GO

145
Black wins the exchange

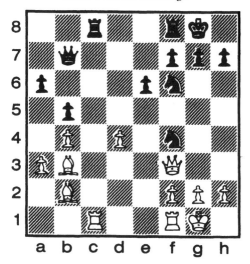

Continuing from Diagram 145, even with the White queen having gone to f3, material will still be lost. First Black takes the f3-queen with the b7-queen, and White recaptures at f3 with the g2-pawn.

The e2 square is now unguarded, White's queen having been removed from the board. The invasion by the Black f4-knight continues as it goes to e2 with check. White must get out of check, moving the king to h1 or g2—it really doesn't matter which square the king chooses, for Black's next move will be to capture the White rook on c1 with the marauding knight. Black wins the exchange, gaining a rook for a knight.

IMMOBILITY AND THE ISOLATED D-PAWN

To summarize: The isolated d-pawn is a static weakness, best exploited in the endgame. The side playing against the isolated d-pawn first fixes it as a target by controlling the blockade square. Occupation of the blockade square, ideally by a knight, immobilizes the d-pawn.

The pieces relegated to guarding the isolated d-pawn are immobilized by it, bogged down in passive defense. The isolated pawn's stationary protectors become, in turn, targets of attack. Ripe for exploitation, they fall easily to such tactical exploitation as the pin, for example.

The blockade square is generally in the chessboard's prime real estate sector, located at a strong point in the center. Successfully occupied, it is a powerful launching pad for penetration into the heart of the enemy position.

ISOLATED D-PAWN: STRENGTH

♟ ▓ ♟

In covering the isolated d-pawn's weaknesses so thoroughly, we may have made it seem to be a severe handicap. But that is not always so. The d-pawn possesses an inherent dynamism.

As previously mentioned, the d-pawn's weakness is static in nature; its strengths are dynamic. The strengths, often concealed below the surface, depend on the activity and interrelationship of the pieces, and on the tactical possibilities and threats that can be generated. Bringing these latent resources to the surface requires a deep and penetrating analysis and accurate calculation.

An isolated d-pawn is first and foremost a center pawn. Its location in the center gives it control over crucial squares, as an examination of Pattern A positions demonstrates.

LOOKING AT PATTERN A AGAIN

A glance at Diagram 146 shows that the only pawn in the center is the isolated White d4-pawn. Black's e6-pawn, near the center, is not equal in value to White's d4-pawn.

Black's e6-pawn controls only one important center square, d5, and it is in Black's half of the board. White's d4-pawn controls two important central zone squares, c5 and e5, both in the opponent's half of the board. And under the proper circumstances, the d4-pawn may advance to d5. Therefore, the White d-pawn presents a greater threat to Black than does the Black e6-pawn to White.

146

The d4-pawn strikes at the center squares c5 and e5

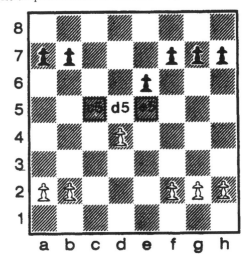

SPACE, WHITE'S FRONTIER

In analyzing the position, consider the amount of space each side has; this allows the calculation of relative piece mobility.

The c-file, which is completely open to both, offers equal chances with no particular advantage to White or Black. On the central d- and e-files, however, White enjoys a small but distinct advantage. White has three squares on the d-file on which his pieces are free to maneuver (d1, d2, d3), and five squares on the e-file (e1, e2, e3, e4, e5). White has a total of eight squares on these two files to use in possible operations.

Black, on the other hand, has only six squares to use on the d- and e-files (d8, d7, d6, d5, e8, e7). White has a clear advantage in space.

The extra space White enjoys, coupled with control of the c5 and especially the e5 outpost squares, points the way for White to make the best use of the isolated d-pawn's strengths. White must play aggressively, keeping his pieces active. The threats White's forces generate will keep Black off balance and prevent the enemy from branding the isolated d-pawn a weakness.

Specifically, White must capitalize on the threatening outposts at e5 and c5. A knight is, of course, ideally suited for occupying these outpost squares. A knight on e5 strikes deep into the marrow of Black's position, continuously threatening to penetrate to several light squares (c6, d7, f7, g6).

WHEN THE QUEENS ARE GONE

In Diagram 147, the queens have been traded. In isolated d-pawn positions, this tends to favor Black, whose opportunities lie primarily in the endgame. But there are still too many pieces on the board for this position to be called an endgame. The remaining White pieces are sufficiently active to give White the advantage. The c1-rook is fully operational, even though challenged by the Black c8-rook for c-file control. Most important, the White knight, seated superbly on the e5-square, looks to invade at c6.

White to play begins by trading rooks at c8, giving check. Black must recapture with the b7-bishop. With that bishop decoyed to c8, the path is now open for White's knight to go to c6, where it "forks" (doubly attacks) the undefended e7-bishop and the undefended a7-pawn. However Black plays, he will lose at least the a7 pawn.

REMOVING THE DEFENDER

Diagram 148 shows a similar invasion of the c6-square. White has succeeded in placing both knights on the outpost squares c5 and e5. That's double trouble for Black.

The c5-knight strikes first, capturing the Black b7-bishop. This removes Black's coverage of the c6-square. Black can capture the b7-knight with either rook—it makes no essential difference. If the b8-rook recaptures, the e5-knight goes to c6 attacking the Black queen and the Black e7-rook simultaneously. If Black retakes with the e7-rook, White still plays the knight to c6, this time forking the

147
The knight invades at c6

148
White to play: removing the guard—invasion at c6

queen and the Black rook at b8. No matter how Black chooses to play, White will win the exchange—a rook for a knight.

JOINING THE TEAM

Two White pieces, the e5-knight and the g5-bishop, team up in Diagram 149. The Black f6-knight, standing guard over the Black kingside, has ambitions of possessing the d5 blockade square. But the knight also has the defensive responsibility of preventing White's e5-knight from coming to d7.

149
White to play: removing the guard—invasion at d7

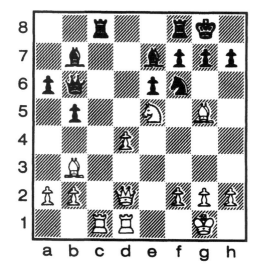

White to move takes the Black f6-knight with the g5-bishop. The e5-knight now has clear access to the d7-square, where it forks Black's b6-queen and f8-rook.

Black has no choice but to allow this. When White plays bishop takes knight, Black must recapture or he will be a full piece down for nothing.

KNIGHT RIPS THROUGH

So far, we've been seeing how the White e5-knight breaks into Black's camp on the queenside, using the c6 and d7 squares. More typical use of the e5-knight is to rip up Black's kingside castled position (Diagram 150).

150
White to play: breakthrough at f7

Black's f7-square is guarded only by the king. If the f7-pawn falls, so will the e6-pawn, since it is doubly attacked by the White queen and the b3-bishop. Tying these two threads together, White sacrifices the e5-knight by capturing the Black f7-pawn. Black retakes with the king (Diagram 151).

White continues as planned, capturing the e6-pawn with the queen and announcing check to Black's king.

If Black now plays his king to f8, White announces instant mate with queen to f7 mate. Black therefore plays his king to g6. White pursues, playing queen to f7, giving check and forcing Black's king to escape to f5 (Diagram 152).

151
White to play: breakthrough at e6

152
White to play: checkmate on the open board

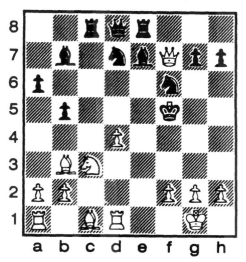

CHECKMATE IN THE OPEN

With the Black king in the open, White now concludes matters by playing the b3-bishop to e6. This is checkmate.

Notice how four White pieces cooperate to remove the Black king's escape squares. The queen covers g6; the e6 bishop covers f5 and g4; the bishop at c1 guards the dark squares f4 and g5, and the c3-knight covers the e4-square. Finally, the isolated d4-pawn eliminates the e5-flight square.

A BIGGER PICTURE

Often, when Black's king-rook is no longer on f8 and is not defending the f7-pawn, White is tempted to take action at f7. In Diagram 153, the action at f7 is part of a larger operation.

153
White to play

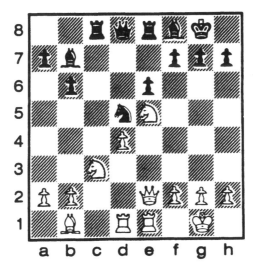

The Black knight's absence from the f6 protecting square is interesting. The knight has jumped too soon to the d5 blockading square and, as a result, the Black king's position is subject to a breakthrough sacrifice.

BREAKING THROUGH

White cracks the Black position by sacrificing the light-square bishop at b1, playing it to h7, where it captures the Black h-pawn with check. Declining the bishop won't help Black, so he plays king takes bishop. Now White's queen enters at h5 with check, driving the Black king back to g8 (Diagram 154).

154
The f7-square falls with check

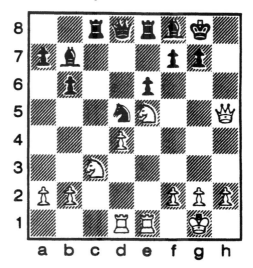

White's queen, backed up by the e5-knight, now captures the f7-pawn with check. Black gets the king out of check to h8. White introduces a new piece, the d1-rook, playing it to d3, where it threatens to deliver a crushing check at h3. Black must pull out all the stops to stave off the mate. Playing the d5-knight to f4 seems a

155
White regains his sacrificed piece

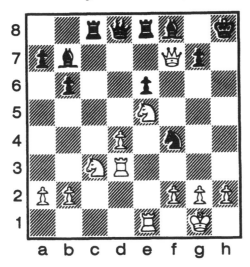

likely try. From here it prevents White's rook from giving check (Diagram 155). But after White's queen captures the knight, Black is behind by two pawns and remains in big trouble.

RECONSTRUCTING RECENT HISTORY

It's easy to reconstruct the recent history of Diagram 156. White has advanced the f-pawn during an attack; when it got to f5, Black traded his e6-pawn for it, and now a White rook stands on the square where the pawn exchange took place.

The exchange has undermined the support of the Black knight posted on the d5 blockade square. White to play continues with the sacrifice of the e5-knight for the black f7-pawn. Black can't afford to take the knight with the king. White would regain the piece immediately by taking the Black d5-knight with the bishop, checking at the same time. Therefore, Black captures on f7 with the f8-rook. Now White removes the f6-knight with the g5-bishop (Diagram 157).

156
Undermining the blockading knight at d5

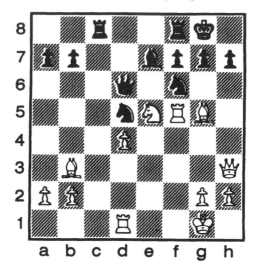

157
A powerful pin on the long diagonal

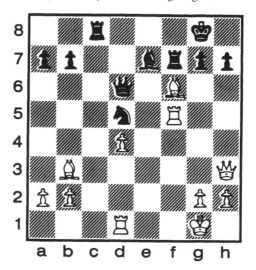

DOUBLE TEAMING

Black's d5-knight is now attacked by White's b3-bishop and f5-rook. Can the knight be saved by capturing White's f6-bishop? Yes, but Black still loses, for White takes the f6-knight with the f5-rook. If Black takes back at f6 with his e7-bishop, then White's b3-bishop takes the f7-rook with check!

HOLD ON!

Black can't bail out of the difficulty in Diagram 157 by taking White's f6-bishop with the e7-bishop. White follows by picking off the d5-knight with his rook, attacking not only Black's queen but the unguarded c8-rook as well—though Black momentarily holds on by playing his queen to c6 (Diagram 158).

158
White wins the house

White's d5 rook now performs a little two-step which breaks down Black's defenses completely. First the rook plays to d6, immune from capture by the Black queen because of the necessity to guard c8. When Black moves the queen to safety at e8, White completes the step by advancing the d6 rook one more square to d7. Black's house falls down since the f7-rook can't be protected in any satisfactory way. Note that, with the queen at e8, the c8-rook can't shift to f8.

A KNIGHT'S HAVOC

To complete the picture of havoc wrought by a White knight against the Black kingside, here is a final example (Diagram 159).

159
Destruction at g6—White to play

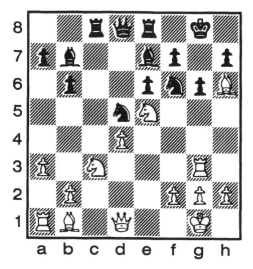

White has five pieces directed at Black's king. Only the a1-rook and the c3-knight are not participating in the assault. The Black king's protection consists almost entirely of a surrounding cordon of pawns, at f7, g6, and h7. Disposing of the Black pawns requires the sacrifice of two White pieces.

First the e5-knight captures the Black pawn at g6. Black retakes at g6 with his h7-pawn. White now offers up the b1-bishop, capturing once again at g6. Black takes the bishop with the f7-pawn (Diagram 160).

160
White applies the finishing touch

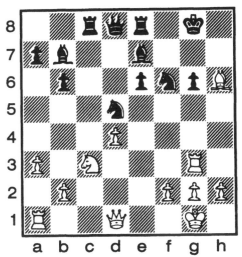

White brings up the heavy artillery, moving the queen to d3, where it takes aim at the undefendable Black pawn at g6. White is threatening to capture at g6 with the queen and give mate at g7. Black can squirm, but he can't save his lost game.

ISOLATED PAWN COUPLE

♟ ♜ ♟

The isolated pawn couple, or couplet, is made up of two pawns connected diagonally, one pawn having advanced one square and the other pawn two squares. They are separated from friendly pawns by at least one file on both sides. Both pawns stand on half-open files yet neither is passed.

The term isolated pawn couple applies specifically to pawns located on the queen-bishop- and queen-files, or the c- and d-files.

Diagrams 161 and 162 show the basic pattern.

THE WEAKNESS OF THE ISOLATED PAWN COUPLE

The isolated pawn couple has a twofold weakness. First, the rearward pawn of the couplet cannot be protected by friendly pawns and is subject to direct threats.

Second, the squares directly in front of the couplet are ideal blockading squares for enemy pieces. Because there are no friendly pawns on either side of the couplet, enemy pieces on these blockading squares cannot easily be driven off. Pieces posted on them are marvelously placed: not only do they prevent any forward movement of the couplet, but they also can impose a total paralysis of the forces defending the unhappy pair.

The isolated pawn couple should be avoided. It has no redeeming features and can paralyze one's game. You will have to misuse your pieces by assigning them to guard the pawns and the squares in front of them.

If your opponent has an isolated pawn pair, try to occupy the squares in front of the pawns, for your pieces would be safe there

161
White has a couplet at c3 and d4

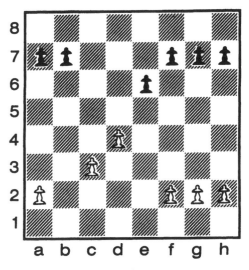

162
Black has a couplet at c6 and d5

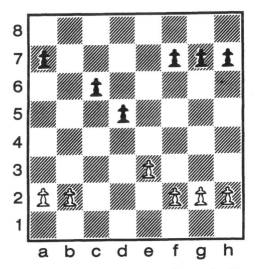

from enemy pawn attack. Place your rooks on the files occupied by the pawns, and use your knights as blockaders. You should have a field day.

KNIGHT CORRAL

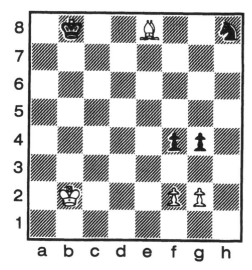

One advantage a bishop enjoys over a knight is its ability to trap the knight without help from other chessmen. A knight needs assistance to trap a bishop. The stratagem for trapping the knight is known as a corral. In Diagram 163, the bishop corrals the knight.

163
The bishop corrals the knight

In this position, the bishop guards the only two squares available to the knight. In the next position, White can set up a winning corral.

The winning move is to place the bishop on e5. From there, all four squares the knight could move to are guarded. After Black's king moves, White advances the pawn to g4 and takes the knight next move.

184

164
White moves and corrals the knight

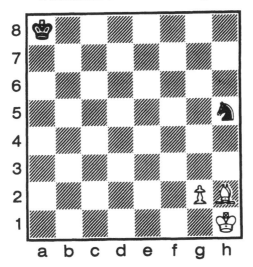

165
White moves and traps the bishop

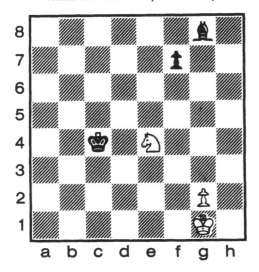

A knight can trap a bishop only if aided by support troops or obstructions. In Diagram 165, Black's bishop can be snared by the knight, for the f-pawn blocks the bishop's escape.

The winning move is knight to f6, attacking the bishop and its only escape square, h7.

Usually, the corral confines the knight rather than wins it. A knight may thus be kept inoperative while the opponent piles up advantages. In Diagram 166, White corrals the knight and then marches the h-pawn to the promotion square.

166
White corrals the knight and the h-pawn queens

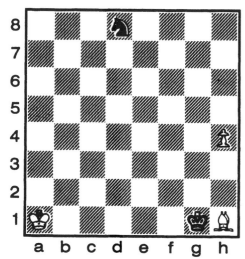

After the bishop stations itself on d5, the knight cannot move without being captured. White's h-pawn then marches unhampered to h8 and becomes a queen.

If you have a bishop against a knight—that is, if you have gained the "minor exchange"—try to use your bishop to limit the enemy knight's scope. Try to corral and win it. If you have the knight, avoid putting it on the edge of the board where its mobility is limited and it can be trapped. Keep your knight centralized and with plenty of options.

MINOR EXCHANGE

The minor exchange is the difference in value between a bishop and a knight. When trading minor pieces, if you wind up with a bishop and your opponent has a knight, you win the minor exchange; if you have the knight and your opponent has the bishop, you lose the minor exchange.

KNIGHTS ARE BETTER IN SPECIAL CASES

Bishops are slightly stronger than knights in most positions, though a knight sometimes shines under the right circumstances.

Knights are better, for instance, if squares of both colors must be guarded. In Diagram 167, the knight on b4 is superior to the dark-square bishop.

This position is a win for White because he can control the corner square a8. This is done by moving the knight to d5 and then to c7.

If White had a bishop on b4 instead (Diagram 168), the position would be drawn, for the bishop cannot guard a8. Black's king is sheltered there permanently, and the game is a draw.

KNIGHTS NEED PAWN SUPPORT

A knight entrenched in the enemy camp is better than a bishop, especially if the knight is unassailably guarded by a pawn. White's knight is clearly superior to Black's bishop in Diagram 169.

167
White wins by maneuvering the knight to c7

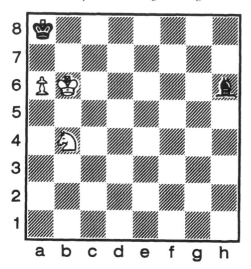

168
The game is a positional draw

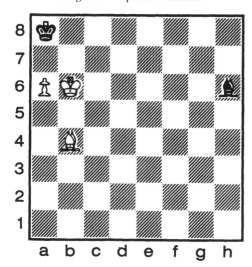

White's knight is solidly entrenched on e6. Nothing can shoo it away. Black's bishop, on the other hand, is passively tied to the

169
The knight gives White the winning edge

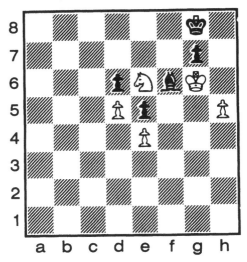

defense of the g7-pawn. White wins by advancing the rook-pawn to h6. Since the g7-pawn can't take it (Black would lose his bishop), White wins the g-pawn and eventually the game.

170
The knight gives White the upper hand

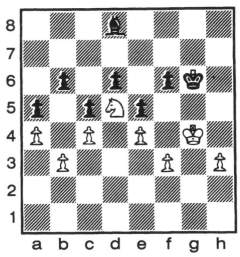

KNIGHTS CAN JUMP OVER OBSTRUCTIONS

Knights outfight bishops in certain blocked positions. Where a bishop has no targets or is completely impeded by pawns, the knight can attack squares of either color and can jump over the barricades and do damage on the other side. In Diagram 170, the knight steps around and over the bishop.

White's knight is strong and Black's bishop weak. The knight has three anchors (b5, d5, and f5), and the bishop is blocked by its own pawns. White can convert this advantage, in conjunction with a superior king position and a passed h-pawn, into victory.

BISHOPS ARE LONG-RANGE TERRORS

But usually, bishops reign over knights. One reason for the bishop's superiority is that it is a long-range piece. A knight must be up close to be effective, and this isn't always possible. A bishop can attack from a safe distance. Diagram 171 shows the long arm of the bishop in action.

171
White wins the knight

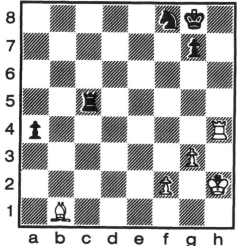

The bishop's long striking power is evident by giving check from a2. Black must interpose the knight at e6, the bishop captures it for nothing, and White is up a minor piece.

BISHOPS CAN MOVE AND GUARD THE SAME SQUARES

Another plus for the bishop is that, if attacked, it can move and still guard many of the same squares. It can keep its eye on a target even if driven back. A knight can't do this. When a knight moves, it guards all new squares. Diagram 172 illustrates.

172
White to move: Black loses a knight

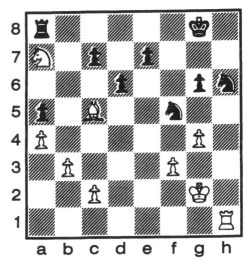

White's bishop and Black's f5-knight are both attacked by pawns, the bishop by the d6-pawn and the knight by the g4-pawn. Each piece guards another friendly piece: the bishop protects the a7-knight and Black's f5-knight defends the h6-knight.

White can retreat the bishop to safety—to f2, for example—

while keeping the a7-knight protected. Black's f5-knight is without that luxury. If it moves to safety, the h6-knight loses its protection and White's rook is free to capture it.

BISHOPS ARE FAST

A bishop is faster than a knight. It traverses the board instantly, whereas a knight needs several moves to get from one part of the board to another. In Diagram 173, White's bishop can get back to g2 in one move to prevent the f-pawn from queening.

173
White's bishop can catch the pawn

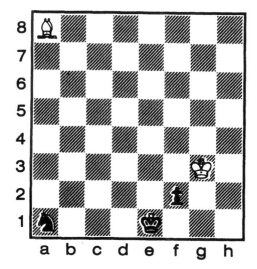

BISHOPS GUARD MORE

A well-placed bishop guards more squares than a well-placed knight. In Diagram 174, White's bishop guards thirteen squares while Black's knight attacks only eight.

174
The centralized bishop has more scope than the
centralized knight

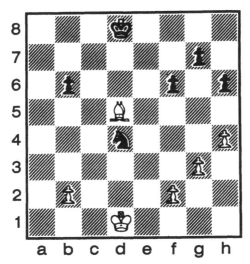

ICE IS ALSO GREAT AND WILL SUFFICE

If you have the choice of trading a knight for a bishop, or a bishop for a knight, evaluate the position carefully. Most of the time, you'd rather have a bishop. Some conditions, however, favor the knight. Try to decide which minor piece is best suited to the resulting position after the exchange.

If you already have a bishop and your opponent already has a knight, try to open the position so that the bishop's diagonals are clear. The bishop is perfect for attacking simultaneously on both sides of the board. A knight's effect is restricted generally to the sector it occupies. Don't weaken your position, for an enemy knight may be able to lodge on a vulnerable square. And don't block your bishop's diagonals with your own pawns.

MINORITY
ATTACK

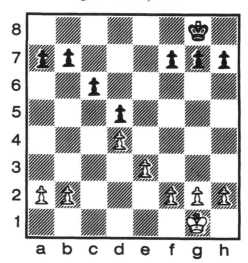

A minority attack is generally an attack by two pawns (the "minority") against three enemy pawns with the idea of forcing a weakness. In Diagram 175, White has a possible minority attack on the queenside. But Black can level a minority attack on the kingside.

GETTING TO B5

The key to White's minority attack is the b-pawn's ability to reach b5, as in Diagram 176. Black's minority attack hinges on getting the f-pawn to f4, as in Diagram 177.

175
White can launch a queenside minority attack, Black a
kingside minority attack

In Diagram 175, White can weaken Black's position by eventually advancing the b-pawn to b5. This can be safely done as long as the White b-pawn is protected so that if it is captured, White can recapture. Once White's b-pawn reaches b5, Black confronts several problems. Black must act, for White's b-pawn threatens to capture on c6.

BRING IN THE ROOK

If, in Diagram 176, Black captures White's b-pawn, the Black d-pawn is isolated and the Black b-pawn exposed to frontal attack along the b-file, especially by a White rook. Diagram 178 reveals a typical position after Black takes on b5 and White recaptures with a rook from b1.

176

The key to White's minority attack is to advance the b-pawn to b5

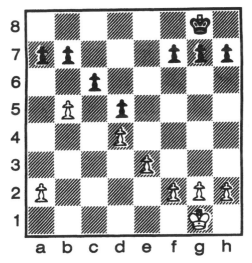

PREVENTING THE ADVANCE

If White is permitted to take the c6-pawn with his b5-pawn, and Black takes back on c6, Black is saddled with a backward c-pawn, as in Diagram 179.

177
The key to Black's minority attack is to advance the
f-pawn to f4

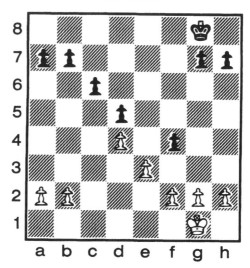

178
White's minority attack has led to the isolation of
Black's d-pawn

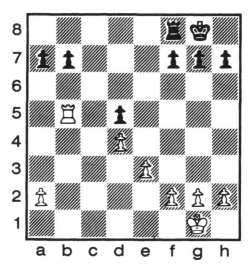

179

White's minority attack has left Black with a
backward c6-pawn

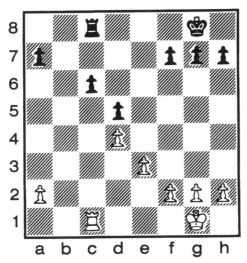

180

Black has stopped White's minority attack, but
accepted a backward c6-pawn

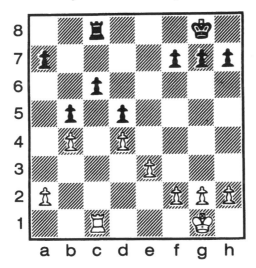

If Black tried to prevent the advance of White's b-pawn to b5 by playing his own b-pawn to b5, that would impair Black's pawn structure: he would still have to guard a backward c6-pawn, as in Diagram 180.

ACCEPTING THE BACKWARD PAWN

Usually, the most satisfactory way to cope with a minority attack is to develop threats that keep your opponent busy elsewhere. Just trying to defend against the minority attack will encourage it and probably enable it to succeed. Passive defense usually leads to positional bankruptcy. The best alternative is to combine defense and counterattack, protecting and attacking simultaneously.

SUPPORT FOR THE ATTACK

Many times it helps to have one or two minor pieces support the minority attack. Rooks, unaided by lighter pieces, are often inadequate.

A White knight on the c5-square, the square in front of the backward c6-pawn, for example, could be quite powerful. And its power would be even greater if it were opposing a minor piece that was helpless to fight for c5, such as a light-squared bishop.

MINORITY ATTACKS IN THE ENDGAME

Minority attacks tend to occur after d-pawn openings, in which, typically, White exchanges his c-pawn for Black's d5-pawn and Black takes back with his e6-pawn. The result is an unbalanced pawn structure in which White has three queenside pawns (a2, b2, d4) opposing four Black queenside pawns (a7, b7, c6, d5). Meanwhile, White has more pawns on the kingside, which is why Black can launch a minority attack on that wing.

But minority attacks can occur also in the endgame. It is useful to relate such themes as minority attacks to the opening variations from which they often arise. This will help you engineer more successful games.

OPENING A FILE

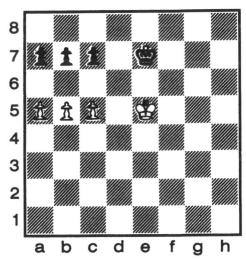

To attack the enemy king, open lines are usually needed—ranks, files, and diagonals with none of your own pawns in the way. Pieces blocked by your own pawns cannot easily develop an attack. To clear obstructed lines leading to the enemy king, try to exchange pawns. Sacrificing a piece is sometimes effective, but since sacrificing can be risky, most of the time exchanging pawns is the ticket.

IT'S EASIER IF AN ENEMY PAWN HAS MOVED

It is difficult to open a file by exchanging pawns if the enemy has not moved a pawn in that sector. For example, in Diagram 181,

181
White cannot open a file without sacrifice

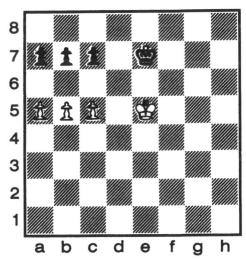

White cannot force the opening of the a-, b-, or c-file without sacrificing a pawn.

But if Black has moved one of those pawns, then it becomes possible to open a file by mere pawn advances. Thus, in Diagram 182, where Black has moved his a-pawn, White can open a file simply by advancing his pawns but without having to sacrifice.

182
White can open the b-file by force

BLOCK THE ENEMY PAWN

To force open the b-file, White must prevent the Black a-pawn from moving. He does this by first playing his pawn from a4 to a5. On the next move, unless White has something more important to do, he should move his b-pawn from b4 to b5.

If Black then captures White's b-pawn with his a-pawn, White can keep the b-file open by taking back on b5 with his rook. If Black doesn't take White's b5-pawn with his a6-pawn, White can still open the b-file for his rook, by taking the a6-pawn with his b5-pawn. The only disadvantage in this case is Black's possible counterplay along the a-file, if he shifts his rook to a8.

THE OPENER MUST BE PREPARED

If you don't block the enemy pawn mass and try to open the file prematurely, the enemy may be able to avoid the exchange. And the result is the file stays closed.

So, in Diagram 182, if White pushes his b-pawn to b5 before moving his a-pawn to a5, Black responds by pushing his a-pawn to a5, keeping the b-file closed.

In Diagram 183, White can force open the b-file because Black has moved his c-pawn.

183
White can force open the b-file

White opens the b-file, not by pushing his b-pawn to b5, which would be met by Black's c-pawn going to c5, but by first pushing his c-pawn to c5 to stop Black's c-pawn from moving. On the next move, White might move his b-pawn to b5. If Black's c-pawn takes White's b-pawn, White's rook can take back, keeping the b-file open. Otherwise, White's b-pawn can capture Black's c-pawn, opening the b-file.

If Black's b-pawn has already moved, White may have several options available to open files, as illustrated by Diagrams 184 and 185.

184
White can force open the a-file

THE TECHNIQUE IS STRAIGHTFORWARD

White can open the a-file in Diagram 184 by moving his b-pawn to b5 and then advancing his a-pawn. If he pushes his a-pawn first, Black's b-pawn could move up to b5, keeping the b-file closed.

In Diagram 185, Black's b-pawn is already blocked by White's b-pawn. White therefore can move his c-pawn to c5 immediately, leading to the opening of the c-file, whether White takes on b6 or Black takes on c5.

In Diagram 186, White seems to have several options, but the only file he can actually open by force is the a-file.

185
White can force open the c-file

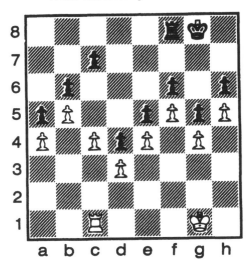

186
White can force open the a-file

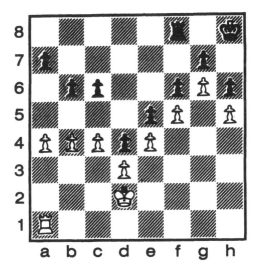

187
White can force open the f-file

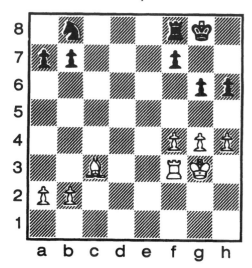

188
White must sacrifice a pawn to open a file

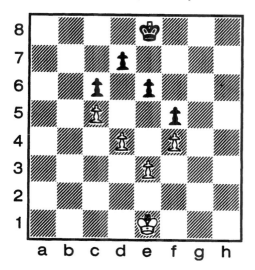

IT DOESN'T MATTER HOW YOUR OPPONENT RESPONDS

White forces the a-file open by pushing his b-pawn to b5, blocking Black's b-pawn. If Black captures on b5, White's a-pawn recaptures, opening the a-file. If instead Black pushes his c-pawn to c5, White plays his a-pawn to a5 and opens the a-file next turn.

If, after White advances his b-pawn to b5, Black defends his c-pawn by moving his rook to c8, White can still march ahead with his a-pawn to open the a-file. Note that Black's rook would be tied to the back rank to stop White's rook from landing there to give mate.

In Diagram 187, White can open the f-file.

White forces open the f-file by first moving his g-pawn to g5, blocking Black's g-pawn. Then, if there are no other tactical situations to deal with immediately, White can move his f-pawn to f5. If Black then takes on f5, White's rook can take back; if Black doesn't take, White can exchange his f-pawn for Black's g-pawn, opening the f-file.

In Diagram 188, White cannot open a file without sacrificing a pawn.

AN OPEN AND SHUT CASE

To sum up, it is much easier to open a file if the opponent cooperates by weakening his pawn structure! Otherwise, you may have to sacrifice material. Before making a breakthrough, it's prudent to back up your advancing, file-opening pawn with a rook or queen. That way, your major piece will be in position to exploit the newly opened file.

The point of all this is the hazard of pawn weaknesses. Avoid them at all costs. Make only necessary pawn moves. If you're not sure of the merit of a pawn move, don't make it.

OUTSIDE PASSED PAWN

An outside passed pawn is sometimes called a distant passed pawn because no other pawns or pieces are close to it. Its chief advantage is that it could become a new queen—or, at least, can be a decoy to lure enemy forces away from the action. Diagram 189 shows White with an outside passed pawn on the a-file.

189
White has an outside passed pawn on the a-file

White's outside passed pawn wins easily by moving straight up the board to make a new queen. Black's king can't stop it.

Diagram 190 reveals how an outside passed pawn can be used as a decoy.

190
White wins, using his c-pawn as a decoy

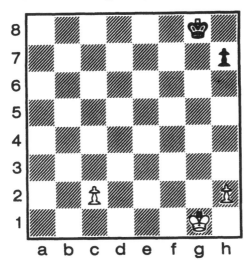

White should first advance his king as far as possible; in three moves, the king can get to g4 while Black's gets to g6, by temporizing as in Diagram 191.

191
White first improves the king's position

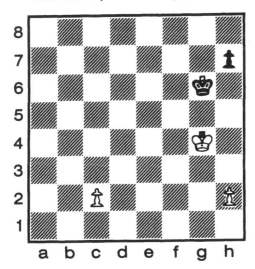

With White's king temporarily stopped, now is the time to use the c-pawn as a decoy. White simply moves it from c2 to c4. If Black doesn't stop this pawn now or soon, it will become a queen.

Black might try bringing his king to f6. But that opens the door on the kingside. Instead of again pushing the c-pawn—it has done its job!—White invades on h5 with the king. Losing the decoy pawn is of no concern to White because he will win Black's h-pawn, clearing the path for White's own h-pawn.

Black's king is powerless to cope with both threats: the advance of the c-pawn and the looming attack on the h-pawn.

It would have been a mistake for White to push the c-pawn impulsively from the start, instead of first improving the position of the White king. For example, from Diagram 190, if White moves the pawn to c4 at once, Black's king moves to f7. If the pawn advances again to c5, then after Black's king goes to e6 (Diagram 192), it's clear that the c-pawn falls. Worse, Black's king gets back in time to prevent White from winning on the kingside.

A possible continuation might be: White's king moves to g2, Black's to d5; White's king to g3, Black takes the pawn at c5; White's king goes to g4, Black's back to d5; White's to g5, Black's

192
Black's king will win the c-pawn and get back in time
to establish a draw

to e6; White's to h6, Black's to f7; White captures the h-pawn, and Black's king goes to f8 (Diagram 193). Now the Black king just shuttles back and forth between f7 and f8, unless the White king allows it to get to the h8-corner. Either way, the game is positionally drawn, for White can't force through the passed h-pawn.

193
The game is positionally drawn

THREATEN TO TRADE PIECES

Outside passed pawns lend themselves to simplifying exchanges. In Diagram 194, the easiest way for White to realize the advantage of his outside passed h-pawn is to exchange off all the pieces. This prevents Black's king from getting over to the kingside soon enough to catch the outside pawn.

If it were Black's move, Black's queen would give mate at a1. But it's White's move, and the cleanest way for White to win is to trade off the rooks and queens. First White's rook on d3 takes the rook on d8 with check, and after Black's rook at e8 takes back,

194
White trades down and queens the outside passed
h-pawn

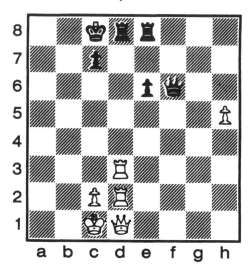

195
Black's king can't catch the h-pawn

White's rook at d2 scoops up the remaining rook, now on d8, again with check. Black's queen takes back on d8, White's queen takes Black's queen, check, and Black's king takes back.

White's pawn then moves to h6 (Diagram 195) and becomes a new queen in two more moves. With no pieces on the board except the kings, Black cannot stop the h-pawn.

THE BASIC STRATEGY

If you have an outside passed pawn, use it as a decoy, but at the right time. Don't advance it rashly. It could fall before you've had a chance to build other advantages, such as a superior king position.

An outside passed pawn is a real plus in the endgame, when your opponent has only a king to cope with it. Therefore, if you have an outside passed pawn in the middlegame, try to trade pieces to reach the endgame. If you are defending against an outside passed pawn, avoid trades and seek counterplay in the middlegame. In this way, your opponent may not be able to utilize the advantage of the outside passed pawn.

OVERSIGHTS

HOW TO REDUCE THEIR OCCURRENCE

If you want to improve your game, the first thing to do is to cut down on oversights and careless mistakes. This is much easier to say than to do, but you really can reduce the frequency of your errors. The way to do it is to play *systematically*.

CONCENTRATE

Achieving total concentration is imperative, though it's very hard to do. In chess, as in any intellectual activity, it's difficult to block out disturbances and maintain your focus.

Try not to be distracted by people, overheard comments, and other games, especially at large tournaments or busy playing areas. During a tournament, you shouldn't get up after each move to tell onlookers how well you're doing. You break your concentration, you disturb other players, and you're probably wrong, anyway.

Some players shut out noise by actually sticking their fingers or earplugs in their ears. That may do the trick. The best way, however, is discipline. Learn how to concentrate. It should benefit all your mental endeavors.

DON'T RELAX AFTER OBTAINING A WINNING POSITION

Tension is often so great during the early stages of a chess struggle that it can be a great relief to know that you finally have a winning game. Naturally, the tendency is to relax a bit, thinking your opponent is on the verge of resigning.

This is a mistake. Never assume that your opponent will resign. No one ever won a game by giving up, so most players fight to the bitter end, just as you do. In fact, some players are at their best when their backs are to the wall. They become more alert as your attention diminishes.

Seemingly hopeless positions actually may contain a dash of poison or one last trap. Relax your guard and you may fall right into it. Good players work just as hard to convert a winning game into a victory as they did to get the winning game in the first place. Remember Yogi Berra's dictum: "It ain't over till it's over."

AVOID RISKY PLAY

Risky moves can backfire. Just because your opponent is inexperienced, don't expect him to overlook a winning counteropportunity. Even if you're facing a newcomer who barely knows the movement of the pieces, don't underrate your opponent's play.

If you take unnecessary chances against ordinary or inexperienced opponents, you develop a slipshod approach that could carry over to more serious contests and cost you dearly.

TAKE YOUR TIME

Don't rush your moves. Don't make automatic responses. Even a position that seems to require a forced response may conceal an unexpected in-between move.

Make sure you understand why your opponent played his last move. Watch out for traps, especially when your opponent plays an obvious threat. Often obvious threats blind us to the possibility of a hidden threat. Expect your opponent to try to set up double attacks. It's the indirect one that usually hooks the fish.

LOOK FOR CHECKS

Sometimes we become so involved in an intricate line of thought that we fail to see the obvious. Take the case of a possible enemy check. Suppose you consider it in your analysis and realize you have an adequate answer. Having analyzed a satisfactory reply on this move, you may think, perhaps several moves down the road, that you still have a reasonable response to it. The conditions that prevailed a few moves earlier, however, might have changed radically—and now the check may be unanswerable.

The same error could rear itself in the analysis of a particular move. When calculating a variation, you could determine, correctly, that you have a good reply to an enemy check or capture. But further along in the analysis, you might neglect to give this possibility a second look. In a slightly different position, the check or capture that you earlier dismissed might be dangerous indeed, but since you've already dismissed it, you might ignore it when you shouldn't, and lose the game as a result.

A check, in particular, can break a sequence. Since you are forced to respond, it can discombobulate your planned variation. So, before introducing a lengthy line of play, before making your next move (even though you've already decided on it), make one last check. Review direct enemy threats—checks and captures—to see if you've overlooked something. It can't hurt.

Be careful. Don't assume anything. Keep a critical eye all the time and watch your play improve.

PASSED PAWN

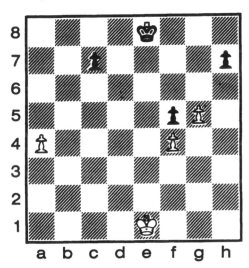

A pawn is passed if it is free to advance all the way to the last rank unhindered by enemy pawns. That means no enemy pawn in its path, no enemy pawn guarding any square along its path.

In Diagram 196, White's a-pawn is passed, and so is Black's c-pawn. None of the other pawns are passed pawns.

196
The a-pawn and the c-pawn are passed pawns

METAMORPHOSIS

The advantage of a passed pawn is that it has a real chance to become a new queen, and an extra queen is almost always decisive. If there are no pawns to stop the advance of the passed pawn, the enemy pieces may have to do it, which diverts them from other actions and responsibilities. And even then, the pawn could promote anyway. If you time the advance of the passed pawn properly, you could frustrate all defensive efforts to stop it.

In Diagram 197, White makes a new queen by simply pushing his passed a-pawn. Once White plays it from a2 to a4, it's off and running. The pawn will queen in four more moves, and Black's king is helpless to stop it.

197
White's passed a-pawn queens in five moves

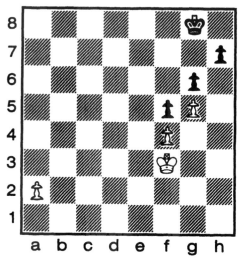

When both sides have a passed pawn, the key factor might be which pawn can queen first. In Diagram 198, both sides queen in the same number of moves, but because White plays first, it is White who wins after promotion.

White queens his pawn on the square h8, and Black on the square b1 (Diagram 199). If White moves first in Diagram 198, he queens first and is then able to give the first check. The new White queen (Diagram 199) checks at h7, skewering Black's king and queen. Once the king moves out of the way, White captures Black's queen for nothing.

198
Whoever moves first wins

199
Whoever moves gains the opposing queen with a skewer

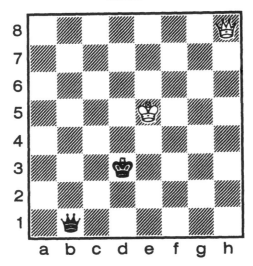

WHO'S ON FIRST

But if Black goes first in Diagram 199, then Black can check White's king from either a1 or b2. This, too, is a skewer. As soon as White's king moves to safety, the White queen is captured without any repercussions.

IN SECLUSION

In your play, try to create passed pawns. Use them to lure away enemy pieces from other duties and activities. But don't push your passed pawn recklessly. That could lose it for nothing. When advancing it, make sure you can support it with other forces and that it cannot be won without your opponent making significant concessions.

Your passed pawns become more important in the endgame and late middlegame, especially when your king is not endangered and can take part actively. Many games often come down to a race between passed pawns. The one who queens first usually wins because his queen can give the first check.

PAWN CENTERS

The central pawn formation is linked closely to strategy. Understand the nature of the center pawns, and you can formulate a reasonable plan. For example, if pawns block the center, attacking there would be like running into a wall. Attacking on one of the flanks would be more promising.

FIVE DIFFERENT TYPES

By convention, pawn centers are classified into five categories: open, closed, fixed, mobile, and dynamic. Open centers have one or no pawns, closed centers have four pawns (two for each side), fixed centers have two pawns (one for each side), mobile centers have three pawns (two for one side and one for the other), and dynamic centers have four pawns (two for each side).

OPEN CENTER

The center is open if no pawns occupy the central files, or if a single pawn occupies one of the middle files but doesn't block passage through the center. Diagram 200 shows an open center.

When the center is open, neither player has time to fool around. Attacks can come out of nowhere, for there are no pawns to obstruct the pieces. Fast development is vital; if your opponent completes development before you do, you could be mated before you could organize a defense. King safety is also crucial. If your king gets caught in the center with no pawns to shield it, you may never reach the middlegame.

200
The center is open

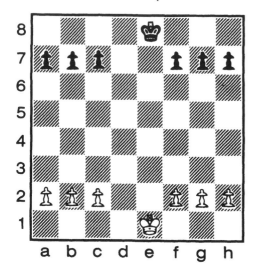

If the center is open, develop quickly and castle early. Before castling, it's especially important not to waste time going for meaningless pawns or threats. Get ready for business first. If you play e-pawn openings, be prepared for open centers. After castling, don't move the pawns in front of your castled king's position. That gives your opponent targets to attack.

Open games are quite tactical and full of sudden turns and surprises. You must be alert at all times, never letting your attention wander.

CLOSED CENTER

In a closed center, each side has two pawns, interlocked and incapable of advancing. With the central files walled up, play proceeds at a slower pace and different principles apply. Diagram 201 shows a closed center.

Since play cannot materialize in the center, both combatants look to the wings for activity. Each player aims for the base of the enemy pawn chain, which in Diagram 201 is d4 for White and e6 for Black.

201
The center is closed

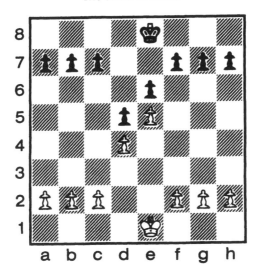

Development does not have to be so rapid. In fact, it can't be. The central barrier inhibits the pieces from coming into play. This also means that the kings are not particularly endangered in the center. They can stay there awhile.

Castling may even be unnecessary. In some cases it might be prudent to keep the king in the center, possibly not castling at all. The center is often safer than the flank in closed positions. Strategy and long-term planning assume great importance. You usually have time to maneuver against your opponent's weaknesses, something hard to do when the center is open.

FIXED CENTER

In a fixed center, each side has one pawn. Neither pawn can move, being blocked or restrained by its enemy rival. Diagram 202 depicts a fixed center.

Fixed centers seem to be a hybrid, combining aspects of open and closed centers; actually, they are played differently from both.

In a fixed center, you try to occupy your strongpoints—the

202
The center is fixed

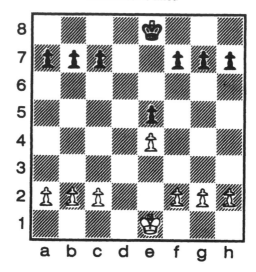

squares guarded by your fixed center pawn. Thus White's pieces should aim for d5 and f5, Black's for bases on d4 and f4. To make the strongpoint secure, you may need to exchange or drive away enemy pieces and pawns that fight for the same squares.

To strengthen a strongpoint, develop rooks to the open file. In Diagram 202, White should position a rook at d1, Black at d8.

If the center is fixed, be careful about making pawn moves. Indiscriminate pawn advances could cost you control of the enemy strongpoint. If White, in Diagram 202, advances the c-pawn to c4, he gives up any opportunity to guard d4 with a pawn. Make good use of your strongpoints and you'll get the edge.

MOBILE CENTER

If you have two connected, movable pawns in the center, and your opponent has a single pawn, you have a mobile pawn center. Diagram 203 shows a mobile pawn center for White.

White's center is mobile, which means it's capable of moving,

203
White has a mobile center

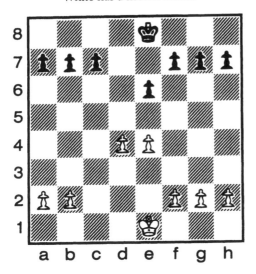

one pawn supporting the other. Having more pawns in the center means that White can control that region.

Black hopes to attack the White center and force it into premature advances, enticing the mobile pawns into indefensible situations. Before White advances the mobile pawns, he must make sure the squares in front of them are guarded. Enemy forces should be driven back or rendered ineffectual. After securing the route in front of the pawns, White may mobilize the center to create a passed pawn. If Black is to attack White's center, he must first win the battle for the squares in front of it. All this leads to a tense struggle.

DYNAMIC CENTER

A dynamic center has two pawns for each side. Diagram 204 shows a dynamic center.

A dynamic center is one whose form will inevitably change. It will, according to circumstances, become one of the other four types of centers.

204
The center is dynamic

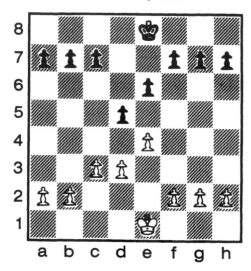

For example, both sets of d- and e-pawns could be exchanged, leading to an open center. A closed center will result if White's e-pawn advances to e5 and his d-pawn to d4.

Exchanges could produce a fixed center. If White's e-pawn captures Black's d-pawn, Black's e-pawn captures back, and White advances his d-pawn to d4, the center is fixed. Another fixed center results if Black's d-pawn takes White's e-pawn, White's d-pawn recaptures, and Black pushes his e-pawn to e5.

A mobile White center appears if White moves the f-pawn to f3, Black's d-pawn captures White's e-pawn, and White's f-pawn takes back on e4. After White pushes his d-pawn to d4, the center is mobilized.

If the center is dynamic, steer the game into the center most favorable for you. Stay alert so you can make the right decision at a moment's notice.

SUMMARY

At some point during the transition from the opening to the middlegame, sit back and determine the character of the pawn center. If the center's open, develop quickly, get your king to safety, and don't waste time. If the center's closed, start preparing to attack on the flanks. Look to undermining the base of the enemy pawn chain.

When the center's fixed, maneuver to occupy your strongpoints and to keep the enemy pieces out of his. If you have a mobile center, first prepare to advance it and then do it. If your opponent has a mobile center, try to get him to advance it before he's ready.

And if the center is dynamic, direct the flow of play to get the type of center that gives you the greatest advantage.

For practice, classify the center of every chess position you see. Developing this skill is vital to your understanding of positional chess and grand strategy.

PAWN CHAIN

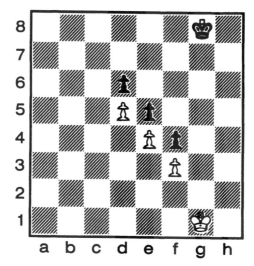

A pawn chain is a diagonal line of at least four blocked and interlocked pawns, two per side. Each pawn in a chain, except the rear one for each side, is defended by a friendly pawn.

If the pawn chain is in the center, the game is closed and slow, for movement is blocked through the middle. Diagram 205 shows a pawn chain.

205
A pawn chain

Aron Nimzovich (1886–1935) developed some basic concepts about pawn chains in his writings. It was important, he wrote, to attack the pawn chain at its weakest link. But it is harder to attack something that can move than it is to attack a fixed object. For this reason, Nimzovich would not have classified the four pawns for each side in Diagram 206 as being a true pawn chain.

206
Constituents of pawn chains

Obviously, the pawns for each side are arranged in two interlocking lines. But in a true pawn chain the pawns at g2 and c7 would not be present. Remember, a pawn chain consists of *blocked* and interlocked pawns that are fixed and cannot move. The c7-pawn and the g2-pawn aren't part of the pawn chain because they can still move.

Attack the pawn chain at its base, which is the part of the chain closest to the enemy's first rank. In Diagrams 205 and 206, White's base is f3 and Black's is d6. The pawns at c7 and g2 in Diagram 206 are *not* the bases of their respective side's chain because they have the ability to move forward.

If the base of a pawn chain falls, the whole chain is weakened because its foundation is undermined. Unless there is a particular reason to attack the head of the pawn chain, the base should be your target.

CLOSED POSITIONS

Central pawn chains usually make the position a closed one. Some openings, such as the French Defense, tend to develop central pawn chains. In the French Defense, White moves his e-pawn from e2 to e4, and Black moves his from e7 to e6. Then White's d-pawn advances from d2 to d4, and Black's from d7 to d5. Diagram 207 shows this position.

207
The first two moves of a standard French Defense

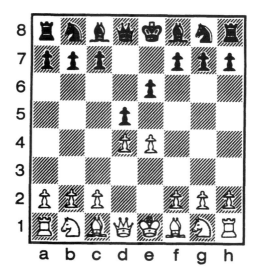

White's e-pawn is threatened by Black's d-pawn. Among several reasonable options, White can protect the e-pawn with a piece, exchange it for Black's d-pawn, or push the e-pawn to e5, out of attack, as shown in Diagram 208.

208
In the Advance Variation of the French Defense, the
central pawn chain makes it a closed position

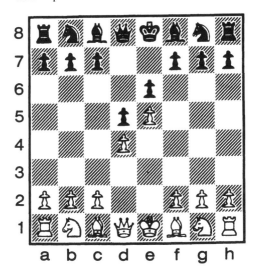

In this position, the center is blocked by the pawn chain, so no real action is likely there for some time.

Since White's pawns are farther advanced than Black's, White has more space, which means he has more room in which to move pieces behind the lines or behind the central pawn chain.

Notice Black's light-square bishop on c8, which is blocked by its own pawn on e6. Restricted in this way, it is referred to as a "bad" or "problem" bishop. Many openings are associated with specific problems for one side or the other; in the French Defense, it's Black's light-square bishop.

Although White's pawns are farther advanced and his position roomier, there's a drawback to having the farther-advanced pawns. The farther advanced they are, the closer they are to the enemy's own pieces and, hence, the easier they are to attack. For example, Black can easily attack White's chain by simply moving the c-pawn from c7 to c5 (Diagram 209).

209
Black's c-pawn attacks the base of White's pawn chain

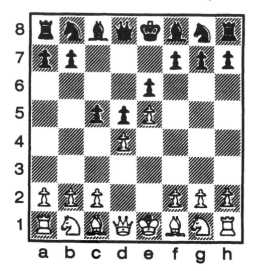

What should White do? If he captures the enemy c-pawn, Black can recapture on c5 with the f8-bishop. And by taking on c5, White voluntarily trades away the base of his pawn chain, weakening his own e-pawn. If the e5-pawn should be traded away or lost, Black will probably be able to advance his own e-pawn later, clearing the diagonal for the development of his imprisoned bishop on c8. What this means is that White should find a way of maintaining the base of his pawn chain on d4.

KEEPING THE CHAIN INTACT

White might try to keep the pawn chain intact by moving his c-pawn from c2 to c3 (Diagram 210).

White's c3-pawn backs up the d-pawn. If Black captures White's d4-pawn, White can take back with his c3-pawn, and the structure of the pawn chain is kept intact, as shown in Diagram 211.

210
White's c3-pawn supports the pawn chain

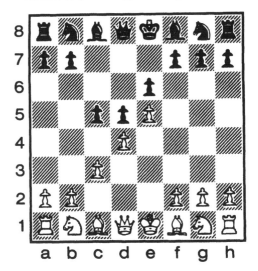

211
White has upheld the base of his pawn chain at d4

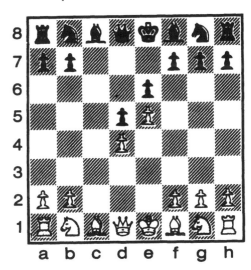

ANGLING TO ASSAULT

White has a fine position, but he shouldn't relax. For example, suppose Black continues by developing the knight from b8 to c6, and White follows suit, transferring the g1-knight to f3. Black could then play his other knight from g8 to e7, and White might plant the light-square bishop on e2 (developing it to d3, to guard f5, would be better here). Black could then shift the e7-knight to f5.

Two black pieces are now attacking the pawn at d4, but it's also defended by two pieces (the f3-knight and the queen), so it's still safe from capture.

If White now castles, the position of Diagram 212 is established.

212
Black to play can win a pawn

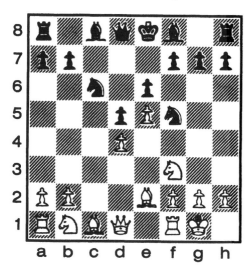

It is Black's move. By shifting his queen to b6, Black assaults the base at d4 with a third piece. White needs a third protector to safeguard d4, and only the c1-bishop satisfies that requirement: Moving it to e3 guards d4.

There are two problems with that: one, the bishop on e3 would be subject to capture by Black's f5-knight. Two, and worse, is that White would be abandoning his b2-pawn, which could be taken by Black's queen (Diagram 213). White might have *some* compensation for sacrificing the b-pawn—he's slightly better developed— but perhaps not enough to justify the loss of a pawn.

213
White has sacrificed a pawn to maintain d4

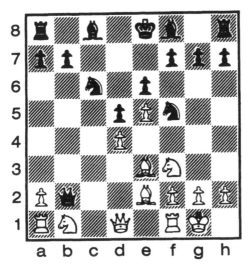

ATTACK THE BASE

A pawn chain's interlocked diagonals of Black and White pawns prevent mobility. If the chain is in the center of the board, the position is closed and the game develops at a slower pace.

To attack enemy pawns in the chain, direct your weapons at the enemy base, that pawn closest to the enemy's first rank. You might begin by hitting the base with an adjacent friendly pawn, offering a pawn trade.

Curiously, Black often can attack White's base before White can attack Black's. The reason is that the White pawns tend to be more advanced and closer to the opposing camp.

SUPPORT YOUR FRIENDLY ASSAILANT

When attacking a pawn chain, try to support your attacking pawn with minor pieces, especially knights. Your queen might be able to join the festivities, too. In closed positions, rapid development often takes a back seat to maneuvering to attack key points and pawns. When the center is blocked, the king can safely remain in the center longer than it can in open positions, and your queen may be able to move about without fear of being ambushed.

The attacker should try to trade off the defender's pieces that are needed to maintain the base. The defender should try to eliminate the attacker's pieces that are endangering the pawn chain. If the pawn chain can be maintained, most likely the side with the more advanced pawns will end up with the advantage. But if the chain is undermined, the advantage is likely to shift to the player who does the undermining.

PAWN MAJORITY

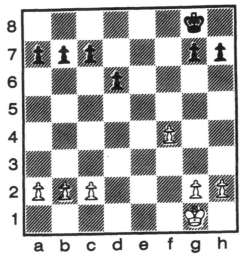

A pawn majority is an advantage in pawn force. You have a pawn majority if, in a specific group of consecutive files, your own pawns outnumber the enemy's. In Diagram 214, White has a kingside pawn majority and Black a queenside pawn majority.

214
White's majority is on the kingside, Black's on the queenside

TYPES OF MAJORITIES

Majorities are generally classified as kingside (comprising the files e through h) or queenside (files a through d). Majorities can occur, however, over a smaller range of two or three files. Central majorities on the d- and e-files are quite common. In Diagram 215, Black has a central pawn majority.

215
Black has a central majority and White a queenside
majority

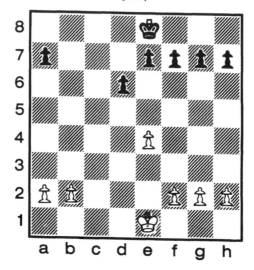

HOW THEY COME ABOUT

Majorities usually arise by exchanging pawns or pieces. If you capture an enemy piece and your opponent takes back with a pawn, that pawn is shifted to a new file. In fact, a transaction like this could create two majorities—one for your opponent on the side to which his pawn shifted, and the other for you, on the other wing or in the opposite direction. Diagram 216 illustrates.

EVERY CAPTURE AFFECTS YOUR PLAN

How does Black take back? The two possibilities lead to different circumstances and plans; either way may be fine in an actual game.

If Black takes back with the d-pawn, capturing "away from the center," he obtains a queenside majority. Between the a- and d-files, he will have four pawns to White's three. In turn, White derives a kingside pawn majority, with four pawns to Black's three between the e- and h-files. Furthermore, White's kingside majority is entirely healthy (no isolated or doubled pawns), while Black's includes potentially harmful doubled c-pawns. Diagram 217 illustrates.

216
White has just captured a knight on c6

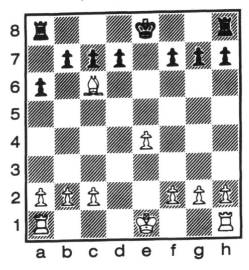

217
Black has captured away from the center; White has a
healthy kingside majority

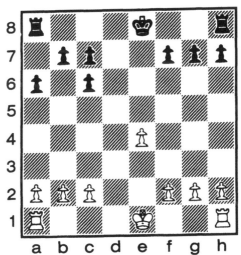

Black could also capture with the b-pawn, "toward the center,"
as shown in Diagram 218, in which case neither side obtains a
queenside or kingside pawn majority. Black winds up with an

isolated a-pawn, however, which will be a real weakness in the endgame. As compensation, he gets an open b-file for a rook and greater control of the center, especially of the square d5.

218
Neither side has a good majority

CAPTURE TOWARD THE CENTER

By capturing toward the center rather than away from it, you get greater central control and avoid giving your opponent a healthy majority on the other wing. These advantages explain the existence of a general principle: *capture toward the center,* even if you have to accept isolated or doubled pawns. It can be crucial to stop your opponent from obtaining a favorable pawn realignment.

OUT OF MAJORITIES COME PASSED PAWNS

A healthy pawn majority—one in which there are no pawn weaknesses and in which every pawn occupies its own file—is significant because it leads to the creation of a passed pawn. This possibility has more impact in the final stages: the late middlegame, the transition to the endgame, and the endgame. A healthy majority in the concluding phase is often decisive. You should avoid exchanges that give your opponent such an advantage. In Diagram 219, White's kingside majority produces an outside passed pawn and wins.

219
White to move creates a passed h-pawn and wins

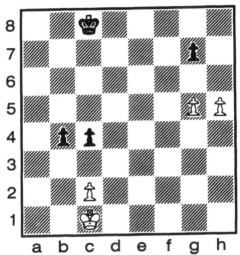

QUEENSIDE MAJORITY

If both players castle on the same side, a majority on the opposite side can be decisive. Since both players usually castle on the kingside (to get the king to safety one move faster), a queenside majority usually is a tangible advantage.

A queenside majority can produce a passed pawn outside the main theater, away from both kings. This could compel the enemy king to waste time hurrying to that side to deal with the looming passed pawn while abandoning the other wing.

In the middlegame, try to mobilize your majority before your opponent activates his. Use your extra pawn for attacking purposes, to open lines and drive back the enemy pieces. In the endgame, use your majority to create a dangerous passed pawn that threatens to make a new queen. Remember the maxim: Passed pawns must be pushed.

POSITIONAL CHESS

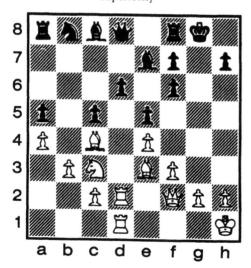

Each advantage, no matter how small, is important because a few small advantages added together can mean a winning position. Steinitz called this the *accumulation theory*. If you play to accumulate small advantages, you're playing "positional chess."

Examples of these small positional advantages include control of the central squares, good pawn placement, early development of the pieces, control of open files, development of knights before bishops in the opening, trading two knights for two bishops in the middlegame, and others.

Consider Diagram 220. White has a won game due to several accumulated advantages spread across the entire board.

220
White to move has overwhelming positional
superiority

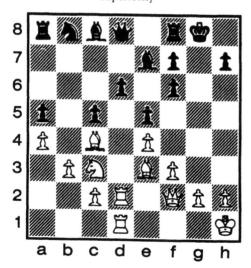

THE TIME FACTOR

Evaluating this position shows how marked White's advantages are. White is well ahead in piece development; all White's pieces are deployed and ready for action. Black, on the other hand, isn't completely developed yet. His entire queenside complement— knight, bishop, rook, and queen—are still sitting on their original squares.

Advantages in development imply a superiority in *time*. Time is measured also in terms of *initiative*, or the ability to control the flow of play.

If you have the initiative, you can attack and compel your opponent to defend. Having the freedom to determine the course of the game usually means having the initiative.

PAWN WEAKNESSES

White's pawn structure is clearly better than Black's, constituting a positional advantage. White's pawns are arranged in two groups, or "islands": the queenside group at a4, b3, and c2; and the kingside group at e4, f3, g2, and h2. Black's pawns are in three groups: one island at a5; another at c5, d6, e5, f6, and f7; and a third at h7.

The fewer pawn islands you have, the easier it is to defend your pawns. You want as few islands as possible. White's two islands here are stronger than Black's three.

Black also has specific pawn weaknesses: the two isolated pawns at a5 and h7. If attacked, these isolated pawns must be defended by pieces, since neither can be defended by a pawn.

Black's f-pawns are doubled. The one at f7 is blocked by the one at f6.

Black has a backward pawn, too, at d6. Its mobility is hindered by White's domination of d5, the square immediately in front of it. Furthermore, the backward d6-pawn is subject to massive attack, especially along the half-open d-file, now occupied by two White rooks.

Black's pawns are badly arranged and are unable to guard a number of key squares, which are therefore weak. If White's pieces occupy these weak squares, Black will be helpless to drive them away, since he has no pawns to do it with. Black's weak squares are a6, a5, b5, c6, d5, f5, f6, h5, and h6. None can ever be guarded by a pawn. Conversely, White has no significant pawn weaknesses for Black to exploit.

THE SPACE RACE

Another positional plus for White is his superiority in space. White's better-placed pieces control more of Black's half of the board than Black's pieces control of White's half.

Piece for piece, White's forces are more mobile than Black's. White's knight attacks the center; Black's is still on the back rank. White's dark-square bishop radiates toward both the kingside and the queenside; Black's is imprisoned at e7. White's light-square bishop is posted powerfully at c4, viewing the queenside and pinning the f7-pawn to Black's king; it cuts right through the center. Black's light-square bishop, though unobstructed, is undeveloped and therefore not playing a meaningful role.

MAJOR PIECES

White's rooks are doubled threateningly on the d-file, attacking in tandem, the advance rook backed up by the rear guard. Black's rooks, by contrast, have a combined mobility of three squares. The f8-rook can move to e8, and the a8-rook can move only to a7 or a6.

White's queen is lethally poised at f2, where it supports the queenside attack of the e3-bishop and is prepared to shift to the kingside along the e1-h4 diagonal with deadly consequences. Black's queen, meanwhile, occupies its original square and has no immediate potential for attack or aggressive action.

WHAT ABOUT THE KINGS?

Finally, compare the positions of the respective kings. White's is safely tucked away in the corner. It is well protected by pawns, and Black is not nearly ready to threaten it.

Black's king position is compromised. The g-file pawn cover is missing, so the king can be checked along the g-file by White's queen. White's bishop can infiltrate to h6, seizing the g7 square for possible mate by White's queen.

WHITE'S AHEAD ON POINTS

In summary, White has accumulated advantages in every aspect of play except material. Both sides have the same kind and number of chessmen. The totality of White's positional advantages, however, is overwhelming.

If it's White's move, playing the knight to b5 (Diagram 221) leads to the quick win of the d6-pawn. Black needs another protector for that pawn but none is available.

221
White wins the backward d6-pawn

White actually has a much stronger continuation in the position of Diagram 220: moving the e3-bishop to h6 (Diagram 222). This invasion threatens the rook at f8 and prepares a crushing check at g3 by White's queen. From g3 the queen can shoot to g7, delivering mate.

So Black must at least allow his rook to be taken by the bishop, a loss of material.

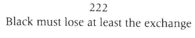

222
Black must lose at least the exchange

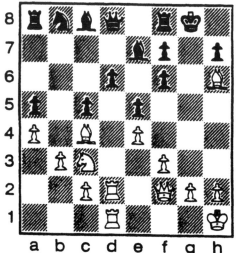

COLLECT ADVANTAGES

In your games, try to accumulate advantages. Build up your position gradually. Play to control the center. Avoid weakening pawn moves. Develop all your pieces quickly and pointedly. Safeguard your king by castling early. Activate your rooks, placing them on open and half-open files where possible. Double them on one of those files.

Play positional chess. Seize open diagonals with your bishops. Induce weaknesses in your opponent's camp, then use them to launch an invasion. The weight of your accumulated advantages will be too much for your opponent to bear. Do all these good things and there'll be many victories in your future.

PROTECTED PASSED PAWN

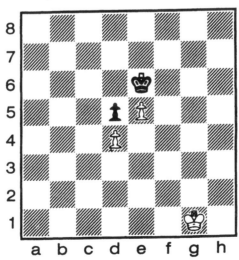

A protected passed pawn, because it is protected by a friendly pawn, is immune to capture by the enemy king, and enemy pieces cannot capture it without being captured back. Diagram 223 shows a protected passed e-pawn.

223
White's protected e-pawn is safe from capture

White's e5-pawn is passed because no enemy pawn can stop its march to the promotion square, e8. Although the Black king can interfere with the pawn's progress, the king cannot capture the pawn while it is guarded by a pawn.

If Black should try to undermine this protection by moving his king to f5 and then to e4, hoping to capture the d4-pawn, White's e-pawn would queen in three moves—Black's king would be unable to stop it. This means that while White's king is free to maneuver around the board, Black's king is tied to defense. In most similar cases, such an advantage is decisive.

Even the presence of other pieces may not reduce the strength of a protected passed pawn. In Diagram 224, for example, White's protected passed pawn at d6 insures a win.

224
White's protected passed d-pawn wins

Black's problems in Diagram 224 are insurmountable. He has a bishop for knight, usually an advantage, but in this position the knight is better. In fact, the bishop doesn't have a safe move.

Black's king lacks power, too. It's confined to the central files, having to guard d7 against an advance of White's d-pawn supported by White's powerhouse knight. This gives White's king carte blanche to maneuver anywhere on the board. Among White's winning approaches is simply to deploy his king at g7, a plan that Black can't stop because his king has to guard d7.

Once White's king occupies g7, even if Black's king is then at e8, White pushes his d-pawn. This sacrifices the d-pawn and forces the exchange of bishop for knight, but then White will win first the black f-pawn and then the black e-pawn. White will soon promote his own e-pawn and win.

Even if Black's bishop were better placed to begin with, say at b5 instead of c8 (Diagram 225), White would still win in the same way.

225
White's protected passed d-pawn insures the win

Protected passed pawns are so powerful that it is not uncommon for a player to sacrifice a pawn to create one. In Diagram 226, Black is threatening to post his bishop on the a7-g1 diagonal. Progress for either side would then be difficult.

226
White sacrifices to create a protected passed pawn

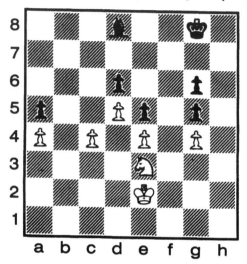

227
White has a winning game

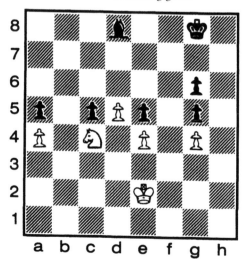

White frustrates Black's plan by pushing his c-pawn to c5. After Black's d-pawn captures on c5, White's own d-pawn becomes a protected passed pawn. White's knight moves to c4 (Diagram 227), a terrific post from which to attack Black's weak pawns at a5 and e5 while also keeping watch over d6, the next square White's passed d-pawn must pass over toward queening.

If Black's bishop now protects the undefended e5-pawn by moving to c7, White pushes the d-pawn to d6. Where can the bishop go? If it moves back to d8, the knight simply takes the e5-pawn, and White ends up with connected passed pawns. If the bishop retreats to b8, we arrive at the position of Diagram 228.

228
White to move

White marches ahead with the d-pawn to d7, threatening to make a new queen. Black's bishop must play to c7 to guard d8. Since now the bishop cannot afford to allow the d-pawn to queen, White's knight captures on e5. If Black's king rushes to f8 to assist the bishop, the knight invades on c6 (Diagram 229), guarding the promotion square (d8) and the Black king's path to stop it (e7). Black will have to sacrifice his bishop for the promoting d-pawn. With an extra piece, White will have no trouble winning Black's pawns and then promoting either his a- or e-pawn. Black is lost.

229
Black is lost

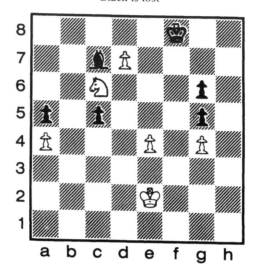

PROTECT YOURSELF

A protected passed pawn is an advantage. It ties down the enemy king and other pieces, allowing your own king and other pieces greater freedom and mobility. Try to create protected passed pawns for yourself and try to prevent your opponents from creating them.

If you have a protected passed pawn, seek exchanges and head for the endgame. If your opponent has such an advantage, avoid trades, keep the game complicated, and try for counterplay. The best way to prevent your opponent from realizing an advantage is to create advantages of your own. Give him something to worry about.

TWO BISHOPS

♟ ♘ ♟

If, in the middlegame, you still have both of your bishops on the board and your opponent has only one bishop or none at all, you have the "two bishops" advantage.

Two bishops tend to be stronger than a bishop and knight or two knights. But this is true only when the bishops are working together harmoniously. If the bishops complement each other, they constitute a small but definite positional plus. A dark-square bishop by itself guards only dark squares, so the light squares might be vulnerable. But if the dark-square bishop is joined by its light-square counterpart, all squares can be covered.

CONTROL OF THE CENTER

Two bishops usually can control the center more effectively than two knights and somewhat better than a bishop and knight. A knight has to be nearby to exert influence, but a bishop can reign over the central zone from afar. Two bishops cooperating can rake the center in the same direction or by crisscrossing it. In Diagram 230, White's bishops guard the center and attack the knights simultaneously.

230
Two bishops attack the center and the knights at the same time

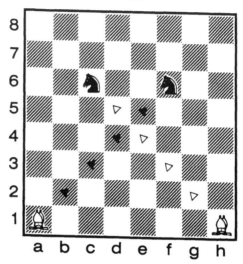

231
The knights are trapped

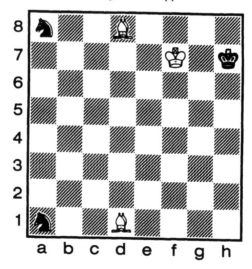

GUARD MORE SQUARES

Bishops also can do a better job of restricting enemy movement than a bishop and knight or two knights can. Bishops are particularly effective in preventing knights from moving safely. In Diagram 231, both knights are trapped.

LONG-RANGE TIGERS

Bishops, as attackers from far away, are well equipped to induce enemy pawn movements. Pawn moves create weaknesses and holes in the enemy camp, and bishops are excellent at exploiting them. The knight needs a base of operations close to its target; the bishop doesn't.

ENDGAME SUPERIORITY

In the endgame, bishops are fast enough to sneak behind enemy pawns and force them to move and become more vulnerable. Two cooperating bishops can wreak devastation. In Diagram 232,

232
White moves and wins material

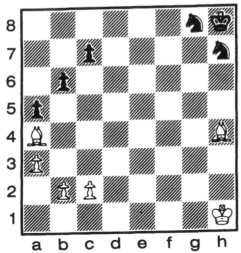

White's dark-square bishop moves to d8 and spears Black's pawns. Black must lose material.

If your king is participating in the action, the two bishops can offer more shelter and provoke entry points for the king. Bishops can also gain time, for example, by counterattacking quickly. This could hamper the enemy's response and restrict his plans.

CAN FORCE EXCHANGES

Two harmonious bishops are also better armed to force favorable exchanges. They can trade from far away, at a move's notice. If you want to simplify to an easier ending and have only knights, it may be somewhat more difficult.

CAN STOP PAWNS

Two bishops are significantly stronger when confronting advancing pawn masses and majorities. If attacked by a pawn, a bishop can retreat and still keep the pawn under observation. If a knight is attacked by an enemy pawn, it may not be able to find a suitable square close enough to keep watch over the pawn. In Diagram 233, White's bishop corrals Black's knight and stops the advance of Black's connected pawns.

PERFECT ESCORTS

Finally, two bishops are perfect convoys for a passed pawn advancing up the board. The bishops guard consecutive diagonals in the pawn's path, and from a safe distance. Two knights, on the other hand, generally have difficulty working in unison. They must be close to be effective, and that may not be possible. In Diagram 234, the knights are helpless to stop the direct march of White's a-pawn.

233
Black has few options

234
White's a-pawn will queen

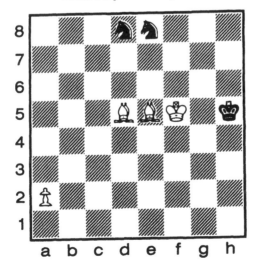

In your games, definitely try to play for the advantage of the two bishops. Be ready at all times to exchange knights for bishops, unless you see that the resulting position is suitable for knights, such as when the board is blocked up entirely by pawns. In positions like that, knights can jump over the barricade but bishops are frustrated.

If you have two knights or a bishop and knight and your opponent has two bishops, try to exchange a knight for an enemy bishop. That should at least negate your opponent's small positional edge.

VISUALIZATION

♟ 🨂 ♟

HOW TO GET BETTER AT SEEING
CHESS MOVES IN YOUR HEAD

Good chessplayers need good memories, though highly selective ones. Being able to remember chess moves, to see variations in your head, to calculate sequences, and so on, are not just natural gifts. These abilities can be developed by training and experience.

There are no formulas for developing these skills to achieve mastery. But if you have trouble visualizing chess positions, there are ways to remedy that problem. They won't make you a world-beater, but they can help you visualize more clearly.

TRY TO SEE THE MOVE

When considering a chess move, really try to see and experience it. As much as possible, give it physical significance. Imagine you see the piece actually moving to its new square, and picture its former square as vacant. Try to feel which pieces and squares are attacked. Sense which squares are no longer defended. To do this, you must be completely absorbed in the game. Halfhearted efforts are meaningless.

USE CHESS NOTATION

Get into the habit of saying the moves you are considering in chess notation. (Do this in your head, of course!) Use algebraic notation, unless descriptive notation is helpful in a specific case. For example, it might make more sense to say "rook-pawns often draw" rather than "a- and h-pawns often draw." Saying the move gives you another associative clue for remembering and visualizing.

You might even imagine the move being written on a score sheet—this gives you another peg on which to hang a move and remember it. Eventually, as you gain skill, you won't need such reinforcement. You'll see everything practically perfectly without artificial aids and tricks.

EXPLAIN EVERYTHING

There should be a reason for every move. You should explain (to yourself, in your head) what an imagined move does, why it should be considered. Try to work out its mystery even if you're uncertain. Some explanation is better than none, especially as an aid for remembering and visualizing. The reason for a move is another associative clue, and formulating it instills the game with logic, the very essence of chess. If you can't explain a move, don't make it.

CONCENTRATE

It goes without saying that your mind should be on the game. Be alive to what's actually happening on the board. Relying too much on book knowledge may dull the senses, especially in the opening, where you could play eight or ten moves without thinking. Since you've studied these moves before, more or less, it's easy to play them from memory, without thought. This can be dangerous.

It's ironic that the opening generally deserves more attention than it often receives. Nuances and subtle transpositions can make similar variations seem indistinguishable. If you're relying on your memory, you're not really seeing the chessboard at all. By the time you wake up, you could have an inferior position.

Concentrate especially in the opening. Understand what is happening in the first few moves. Imagine that they are happening for the first time. This will help you see middlegame variations in your head. The logic of the earlier positions will suggest later possibilities.

Use your opponent's time wisely. It's easy to let your mind wander, waiting for your opponent to play a move. But during his time you should be thinking, though not the way you think on your own turn. This is the time for you to investigate more general concerns and features, such as pawn configurations, king safety, weak and strong squares, piece cooperation, converging attacks. All of this information can help you see things better in your head, especially when you organize it around a central purpose. It will enable you to keep focused, and that will help you see more.

LOOK FOR PATTERNS AND RELATIONS

When you consider a piece's placement, imagine vectors extending outward from it along its lines of power. If a rook occupies an open file, sense it driving up the length of a column. If a bishop zeroes in from the flank, feel it cutting the board in half.

Especially when play revolves around a fianchettoed bishop, you might discover moves more easily, and see them more clearly, if you try to develop pieces and pawns on squares where they support the bishop's long-diagonal control.

Picture moves in color and group them accordingly. For example, suppose with the White pieces you have fianchettoed your king-bishop at g2. That bishop fights for control of the a8–h1 diagonal, which consists of light squares. You might think of placing supportive pieces and pawns where they contest or control squares along that diagonal.

It would not be uncommon to see a bishop at g2, Pawns at c4, d3 and e2, and a knight on c3, all working together to control key light squares. You might think, under such circumstances, that you are playing a light-square game. Once again, this stimulates your associative powers and makes it easier to generate and visualize move possibilities.

AN EXERCISE

Try the following exercise under conditions free of disturbance or distraction, perhaps while you're lying in bed, or walking alone outdoors.

Pretend you are sitting on the side of the board. Imagine the square a1 with a White knight on it. Try to mentally construct a position in which the knight being there makes sense.

Next example. Imagine a White knight on b1. Again picture a position in which the knight on b1 is logical. Go around the board, in sequence, making sense of each position for the knight. If you've had extensive experience, try to remember actual games or positions in which such situations actually occurred.

After doing this with the knight, do the same for the bishop, rounding the board and manufacturing logical positions that justify the various bishop placements. Then do this for the rook, queen, and king, in that order. Such an exercise can only improve your skill at visualization and make you a better player.

One overall piece of advice: Try to analyze in your head every chance you get. The more you do it, the better at it you'll become. Practice makes perfect.

WEAKNESS

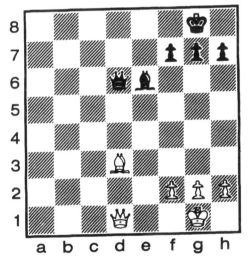

A weakness can be tactical or positional. A tactical weakness is one based on immediate or temporary circumstances. Given time, a tactical weakness can be defended or eliminated: protection can be added, or the threatened man moved to safety.

Diagram 235 shows a tactical weakness.

235
Black's d6 is tactically weak

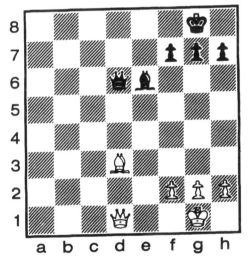

Black's queen on d6 is unprotected. Note that White's queen is also on the d-file, blocked only by the d3-bishop. If it were White's turn, this alignment could be exploited immediately: White would take the h7-pawn with the d3-bishop, giving check, and simultaneously attacking Black's unprotected queen with his own. Since the check would have to be answered, Black's queen would be captured on White's next move.

The tactic used here is a discovered attack, or discovery. If it were Black's move in Diagram 235, moving the queen off the d-file or to a protected square would eliminate the tactical weakness.

POSITIONAL WEAKNESS

When people talk about weakness, they usually mean positional, not tactical, weakness. Positional weaknesses tend to have long-term ramifications. They are not subject to the shifting situation from move to move as are tactical weaknesses. It takes more than a few moves to correct a positional weakness, if it can be done at all.

Positional weaknesses concern pawns. A square is weak if it can't be guarded by a friendly pawn, either because there are no friendly pawns on adjacent files or because the friendly pawns that could have protected the weak square are too far advanced. Sometimes a friendly pawn on an adjacent file, though not too far advanced, may be restrained by enemy pieces or pawns and can't be used to protect the weak square, which therefore remains weak.

TYPES OF WEAKNESSES

If you have a weak square or a weak pawn it is likely to be on your third or fourth rank. Typical pawn weaknesses include isolated pawns, backward pawns, and the isolated pawn pair. Other formations, such as doubled pawns and hanging pawns, though tending to be weak, can, under the right circumstances, possess surprising strength or display other advantages.

Sometimes a weakness results not because the pawns are doubled or isolated but because they all occupy squares of one color. In such instances, the other color squares are weak and subject to enemy occupation. This weakness is accentuated when the enemy has a bishop that is able to travel on the weakened squares undeterred by a bishop of your own.

Let's look at some of these weaknesses.

236
White is weak at e4, e3, and d3

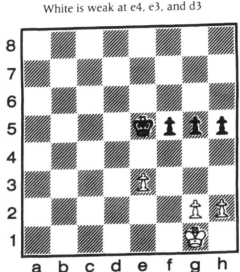

In Diagram 236, White's isolated e-pawn is weak. No pawn can guard it if it's attacked, so White's king will have to do the defensive chores. Two other squares in particular are weak: e4 and d3, on White's fourth and third ranks. White can't guard either square with a pawn, and Black's king may be able to exploit this by occupying those squares.

DOUBLED ISOLATION

In Diagram 237, White has doubled isolated pawns. They are weak because neither can be guarded by a friendly pawn. If they are attacked, only the White king can protect them. Two isolated

237
White is weak at f3 and f4

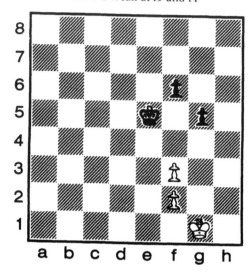

pawns are often not much better than one, and sometimes they even get in each other's way (more on this below).

The squares f3 and f4 are particularly weak for White, and f4 is subject to immediate occupation by Black's king. Black to move would invade with the king to f4. After White's king moves to g2 to defend the f3-pawn, Black simply moves his f6-pawn to f5. White must move, but all he can do is to move the king away from the f3-pawn, which is captured by Black's king for nothing.

ALL CLOGGED UP

This shows how doubled isolated pawns can get in each other's way. If White didn't have a pawn at f2, shifting the king to f2 would have provided adequate defense.

Diagram 238 reveals the best alignment for two friendly pawns.

238
White's pawns are connected; Black's are isolated

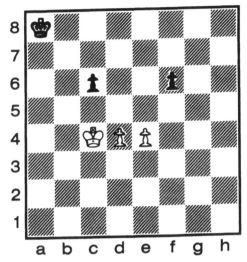

Black's isolated pawns will need defending by the king. The squares in front of each pawn are weak—c5 and f5. White's king will try to occupy these weakened squares advantageously.

White's pawns are connected. The square in front of each is guarded by its friendly partner. If attacked, either of these connected pawns might be able to advance with the support of its neighbor.

White to move wins by occupying the weak c5-square. Black's king then defends the c6-pawn from b7, and White's king invades to d6. Black's f-pawn is then a sitting duck.

PAIRS OF PAWNS

Sometimes pawns occupying adjacent files are connected but lack the ability to advance together. If the squares in front of them are weak and controlled by the enemy, as are the squares in front

239
White's pawns at f3 and e4 are an isolated pawn pair

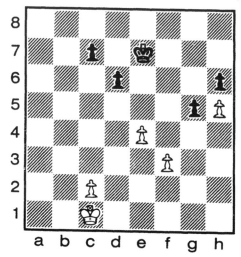

240
Black's king occupies White's vulnerable square

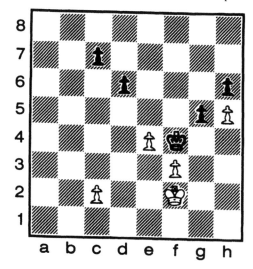

of White's e4- and f3-pawns in Diagram 239, they are an isolated pawn pair. The squares e5 and f4 are strong for Black, weak for White. White must rely on his king—instead of the more natural helpers, pawns—to keep Black's king out of those squares.

White's isolated pawn pair is held in place by Black's d6- and g5-pawns. In Diagram 240, Black's king has already infiltrated.

Black's king has penetrated to White's Achilles' heel, f4. White's king has arrived in time to defend f3, as well as e3 and g3—keeping out Black's king—but White is helpless against the menacing advance of Black's g-pawn.

What does White do after Black moves the g5-pawn to g4? If he moves his king, Black captures his f3-pawn for nothing. If White instead captures Black's g4-pawn with his f3-pawn, Black's king takes back on g4, and White will not be able to save the h5-pawn.

UNCONTESTED WEAKNESSES

241
White's pawns cannot guard e5, f4, g5, or h4

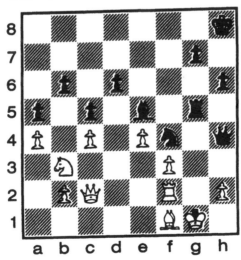

Diagram 241 shows what a powerful game can be developed if you can occupy the enemy's weak points uncontested. Black's queen, rook, bishop, and knight overwhelm White's kingside. White is extremely weak on the dark squares, many of which can't be guarded by pawns, and his pieces don't help much. White is positionally lost; it's only a matter of time before his position falls apart.

A LIGHT WEAKNESS

242
Black is weak on the light squares

In Diagram 242, Black is deficient on the light squares. These can't be guarded well, and some are very important, central on the board and to the position. All Black's pawns are on dark squares, unable to guard light squares. And Black's dark-square bishop can't help.

White has a light-square bishop, and it can capitalize on Black's vulnerability. White's queen occupies g6, a square dangerously close to Black's king. If Black's pawn were on h7, White's queen would not be able to occupy such a threatening square.

White wins by moving the bishop to e4, threatening mate by the queen at h7. If Black's king flees to g8, White's bishop exploits the light squares again, moving to d5, giving check again. When Black's king backs off to h8, White's queen invades to f7, scenting mate at g8. This invasion also threatens the Black bishop at f8. Black must lose material to avert mate.

TURNING IT AROUND

White, in this example, has doubled connected kingside pawns, but they aren't weak. Only pawns that can be exploited by the enemy are weak. If they are safe from attack, they only have the potential to become weak.

In Diagram 242, White's doubled pawn on g3 is an advantage: It provides additional shelter for the king, so that Black's queen can't give pesky checks along the e5-h2 diagonal.

Don't rely too much on generalities in chess. Each case requires individual treatment, like the g-pawns in this position. The exception happens more often than you might think.

PAWNS ARE THE ROOT OF MOST WEAKNESSES

Most weaknesses are caused by pawn moves. Every time a pawn moves, at least one square is weakened, forever unprotectable by a friendly pawn. Granted, some weaknesses resulting from pawn moves are irrelevant in the grand scheme, and the pawn move's virtues may outweigh its liabilities. For example, attacking chances may be gained or open lines favorably created by moving a pawn.

The partial diagrams that follow (without pieces) highlight some kingside pawn moves and their attendant weaknesses. In each case, squares have been weakened or pawns have become targets for enemy attack.

FIANCHETTO: FRIEND OR FOE?

243
White has weakened f3 and h3

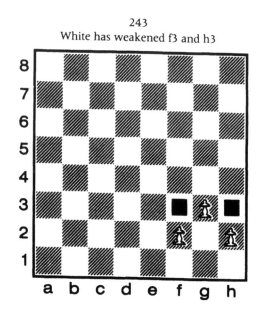

In Diagram 243, White's g2-pawn has moved to g3. This is a natural move if White wants to fianchetto his kingside bishop at g2. But the f3 and h3 squares are irreparably weakened by this advance. They can never again be controlled by a White pawn, and that gives Black's pieces a better chance to occupy them.

White should not allow Black's pieces to post themselves at f3 and h3, so he should keep the light-square bishop on the board, if possible. Then those weakened squares might at least be guarded.

INCLUDE AN ESCAPE HOLE

In Diagram 244, White has made an escape square for his castled king by moving the h-pawn to h3. But this advance has slightly

244
White has weakened g3

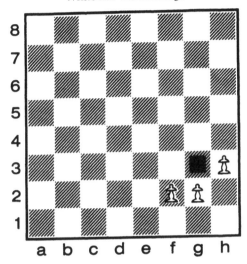

weakened g3—only slightly because it is still guarded by the f-pawn. If Black had a dark-square bishop or queen posted on the a7-f2 diagonal, however, the f-pawn would be pinned to White's king and thus would *not* be defending g3.

White may have moved up his h-pawn to attack a Black knight or bishop at g4, or to prevent one from moving there. Such pawn advances should be avoided on general principles and considered only for a compelling reason.

Remember, once you've moved a pawn, it can't move back. Pawn errors are permanent. Errors with pieces, however, may sometimes be overcome, given enough time to correct them.

WEAKENED SQUARES

In Diagram 245, White has weakened e3 and g3, though g3 is still guarded by the h-pawn. White must now try to prevent Black from exploiting the a7-g1 diagonal, since the f-pawn has moved.

245
White has weakened g3 and e3

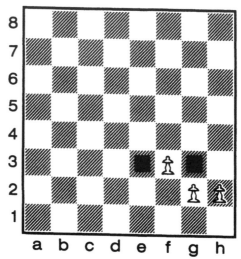

246
White has weakened f3, f4, h4, and h3

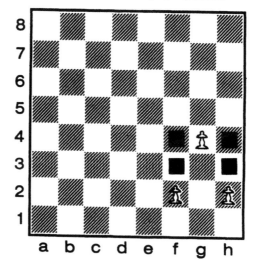

In Diagram 246, White has weakened four squares: f3, f4, h3, and h4. White's pawn advance to g4 in a castled position is among the worst moves possible. Black's pieces can have a field day swarming to occupy these squares in preparation for attacking White's king. The g4-pawn itself is weak and subject to attack.

247
White has weakened g3 and g4

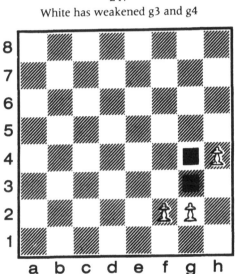

In Diagram 247, White has made another bad pawn move, advancing the h-pawn to h4. The g3-square is slightly weakened, g4 is severely weakened, and the h4-pawn itself is a target of attack. If White defended it with the g-pawn, the position would be weakened even further.

PUSHING TO F4

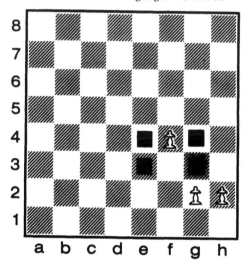

248
White has weakened g3, g4, e3, and e4

In Diagram 248, White has weakened four squares: e3, e4, g3, and g4. After castling kingside, the White king stationed on g1 might also be subject to attack along the a7-g1 diagonal. On the other hand, if there's a White rook at f1, as there often is after castling kingside, the advance of the f-pawn may result in a pawn exchange that opens the f-file for the rook.

Thus, the push f2 to f4 is double-edged. It could prove to be weak, but it also gives White the chance to build attacking possibilities.

WHY OPENINGS AREN'T FOR PAWNS

There is no more convincing argument against indiscriminate early pawn moves than what follows.

White begins by advancing his f-pawn to f3. That is a mistake—it weakens g3 and exposes the e1-h4 diagonal. Black should follow with a vigorous advance of his e-pawn to e5. If White then blunders with the thrust g2 to g4, the Black queen can't be blocked once it moves to h4. White would be mated, just punishment for his two irreparably weakening pawn moves. Diagram 249 shows the final position, called the Fool's Mate.

249
White has fallen for Fool's Mate

TACTICAL AND POSITIONAL SUGGESTIONS

There are tactical weaknesses and positional weaknesses. Tactical weaknesses should be exploited quickly, or your opponent may eliminate them. Positional weaknesses, usually based on pawn structure, are longer-lasting, requiring more gradual methods to exploit.

If your opponent has a partially exposed king, expose it further. Consider a piece sacrifice to break up the enemy king's position. Lacking pawn cover, the king will be vulnerable, the more so if he has no friendly pieces on that side of the board.

If your opponent has an unguarded and exposed piece or pawn, try to win it tactically, especially by a double attack, such as a fork, involving another enemy unit.

Positional weaknesses can be exploited, too. For example, if your opponent has a weak square, post one of your pieces there, especially if your piece can be securely guarded by a pawn.

Fix enemy weak pawns as targets. Prevent them from moving by guarding or occupying the squares to which they might move. If you keep your opponent's pieces busy guarding those weak pawns, those pieces become passive and ineffective.

If your opponent has a weakened king's position because a pawn or two was moved in front of the king, try to open lines leading to the king by moving up your own pawns, trading them off, even sacrificing them. Just make sure that if your own king is castled on the same side it is not endangered by these very advances.

If your opponent has a cramped position, keep it cramped. Don't allow him to free his game by advancing pawns or trading pieces. Let him suffer!

Finally, to reiterate: If your opponent has a weakness, throw everything at it. Exploit it. If *you* have a weakness, divert the enemy by developing a counterattack or turn the weakness into a strength. Most features on the chessboard have dual aspects, strong and weak points. Minimize your weaknesses and emphasize your strengths.

ADDITIONAL CONCEPT GLOSSARY

Attack There are two kinds of attack: specific and general. If you are in position to capture a specific enemy piece or pawn, you are attacking it. Such an attack is not a threat, however, unless you can capture with advantage.

More general attacks consist of a larger assault force and have both immediate and long-term aims. For example, in a kingside attack, several pieces and pawns, working together, might try to induce the opponent to create weak squares around the enemy king's position which the attackers can then occupy. Specific attacks and threats will arise in the course of this overall campaign, the big prize being the enemy king.

Back-rank Mate If you mate the king by checking along your last rank (your opponent's first rank) with a rook or queen, you are giving a back-rank mate. Sometimes the same type of mate is delivered along the a- or h-file (or any file where obstructions prevent the enemy king's escape); this is a "corridor mate."

To avoid the possibility of being mated along your first rank, create an escape hatch for your king. This usually is done by advancing the rook-pawn of the castled position one square; it could also be moved two squares, or the knight-pawn or bishop-pawn could be advanced instead.

Giving yourself breathing space in this way does, however, weaken your pawn structure and create a target for enemy attack. Consequently, as you approach the endgame and the queens are off the board, it might be a better idea to bring the king back to the center than to create unnecessary pawn weaknesses.

Behind a Passed Pawn You have a passed pawn and a rook. Your opponent counterattacks with a rook. The pawn needs support along its route to queening. Though rooks can work in front of or alongside pawns, they work best from behind, for several reasons. *A rook behind the pawn protects it as it advances.* The enemy rook may try to block the pawn's path, especially the promotion square, but rooks by themselves are poor blockaders, so this only signals doom for the defending rook. Moreover, as the pawn marches up the board, the mobility of the rook behind it *increases* as the scope of the rook in front *decreases*.

Change places: You're the defender now. It's still preferable to get your rook behind the pawn. It's folly for the attacking rook to guard the pawn's path in front, for eventually the pawn reaches the seventh rank blocked by its own rook on the eighth rank. Unless the obstructing rook moves away with a gain of time (that is, by making a serious threat), it abandons the pawn to the enemy's rook positioned behind it.

Defending a passed pawn from the side is no better. Since the rook guards the pawn but not the squares in the pawn's path, the pawn advances without support.

To support a passed pawn, put your rook behind it.

Candidate Passed Pawn   Let's begin with the concept of pawn majorities. A healthy pawn majority can produce a passed pawn. In a given majority, the pawn that can become passed is the *candidate*. It is the candidate because no pawn blocks its path, though enemy pawns can restrain its advance from adjacent files by guarding squares along its path.

Not all candidates are equal in value. Generally, the more distant it is from the enemy king, the better. If you can exchange pawns and also shift the candidate further away from the enemy king, do so. Your advancing pawn thereby becomes more of a threat.

Suppose White and Black are castled on the kingside and that White has a queenside majority of two pawns versus one. White's pawns occupy the b- and c-files. In that case, it's better for White if Black's queenside pawn occupies the c-file, not the b-file, for White's candidate is then on the b-file. If Black's pawn occupied the b-file instead, White's candidate would be on the c-file, closer to Black's king. That means the Black king can reach the pawn one move sooner. That one move can make the difference between winning and losing!

Capablanca's Rule   This principle determines which pawn in the majority should move first before the entire majority is activated. The rule is to first advance the candidate passed pawn, which has no enemy pawn obstructing its path. Moving other pawns first could sap the majority of its strength.

Suppose White has pawns on a2 and b2, and Black has a single pawn on a7. White should move the candidate b-pawn to b4 first, and then move the a2-pawn. If White starts with the advance a2 to a4, Black can stymie White by moving the rook-pawn from a7 to a5. Suddenly White's advantage is nullified. The a4-pawn is blocked and the b2-pawn can safely move only to b3.

Remember Capablanca's rule in your own games. *Push the unopposed pawn first.*

Centralization   This principle applies to open positions, in which movement through the center is possible and the middle of the board can be occupied by pieces. It's less relevant in closed positions, where the center generally is blocked by a wall of pawns.

Develop your pieces toward the center. Later, if desirable to centralize them more, move them closer to the center or position them to influence the central zone more effectively.

Centralizing your forces increases their mobility. Centralized pieces radiate in all directions, inhibiting your opponent's development and attack, preventing his use of comparable vantage points.

If you get to the center first, you may not have to supply support for those squares. But it's prudent to reinforce your center. Bring up the troops!

Closed Game   A game is considered closed if the center is more or less blocked by pawns so that movement through the center is impeded. Such positions, where none of the central pawns have been exchanged, slow the pace of the game and contradict principles of the open game.

Development is sluggish because diagonals and files are blocked. There are more pawn moves, especially on the flank. Castling can be delayed, there being no immediate need to safeguard the king behind a wall of pawns—the blocked center already fulfills that function. Play on the wing predominates as fewer opportunities arise to employ the central squares. Knights have more time to maneuver; bishops are less effective because of pawn obstacles. In closed games, players generally try to accumulate small positional advantages. Grandmaster games of this type are often incomprehensible to the average player.

Combination   A combination is a forced series of moves, often involving sacrifice—which leads at least to an improved position. Most combinations gain material or end in mate. They often contain a surprise element and frequently combine several tactical themes.

The crux is the forced nature of the sequence. A combination is hardly possible if you can't visualize how to force your opponent's responses. Only when you know that if you do this your opponent must do that can you play a combination.

If you have the overall advantage, you may have a combinative possibility resulting from the accumulation of positional advantages. Without positional superiority, it's unlikely you'll have a combination. When a position definitely seems to slant in your favor, take care to analyze more deeply. Focus especially on your opponent's weaknesses and tactical vulnerability. How safe is your opponent's king? If it's even partially exposed, and your opponent has other problems, looking hard may unearth a winning combination for you.

Cramped Position   A cramped position is one in which your pieces are blocked by your own pawns and your pawns restrained by enemy forces. If you could only make a freeing move or two with a couple of pawns, your pieces might achieve greater mobility. As it is, pieces and pawns are stepping on each other.

If you have your opponent in a cramped situation and control more of the board than he does, try to keep it that way. Guard the squares in front of his pawns to discourage their movement. And avoid trading pieces. Your advantage derives partly from the fact that his pieces have no scope and yours do. Exchanging pieces helps your opponent to get rid of his problems.

Decoy   An outside passed pawn, or a candidate pawn occupying a distant file, is a decoy. At a timely moment, the decoy can be pushed to lure the enemy king away from its proper milieu. That could leave your opponent's base camp defenseless against your king and other pieces. If you sacrifice the decoy, you may be able to grab several pawns in exchange and clear a path for a passed pawn.

But don't push the decoy prematurely. You don't want to lose it before you've had time to prepare an invasion.

Before committing yourself to a plan or action, be certain you haven't overlooked the consequences. Build your game, reposition your forces, and make sure that when you pull off your plan it *works*.

Discovered Attack   This is a tactic involving two friendly units on the same rank, file, or diagonal. The front unit can be a piece or pawn, but the rear one must be a piece. An attack on an enemy target is discovered when the front unit moves, unveiling the stationary rear piece's line of power.

The success of a discovered attack usually depends on what the front unit does when it moves. It often can move or capture without being captured itself because the discovered attack is so serious—a check, for example—that it requires immediate attention. The moving unit in such cases has virtual carte blanche to get away with anything.

If the moving and stationary units create simultaneous threats, the discovery is a *double attack*. If both attackers give check, it is a *double check*. Try to set up discovered attacks—they can be amazingly effective.

Double Attack   A double attack makes two or more threats with the same move. If one of your units threatens to capture two or more enemy units, it's a *fork*. When two of your units make separate simultaneous threats, this is a *discovered attack*. Yet another double attack is a threat by one of your units to capture an enemy unit and a simultaneous threat by the same unit to give mate. Two different units attacking different targets on the same turn is also a double attack.

Double attacks are tactics. The main double attacks are forks, pins, discoveries, skewers, and underminings. Try to prepare double attacks, especially those that combine direct and indirect threats. Your opponent, seeing the direct threat, may not look any further and miss the hidden threat.

This works both ways. If your opponent threatens you in some obvious way, don't stop looking. Check to see if he's got an additional threat up his sleeve.

The Exchange   If you win a rook (usually valued at the equivalent of five pawns, or "points") but lose a bishop or knight (worth three points), you *win the exchange*. If you lose a rook for a minor piece (bishop or knight), you *lose the exchange*.

If you've won the exchange, the winning strategy is to use the rook's superior mobility to improve your position by reducing your opponent's options to the minimum. At the critical moment, you may be able to sacrifice the rook for a minor piece plus a pawn. You will no longer be up the exchange, but you'll have one more pawn than your opponent, and that can be converted into a queen.

Fork   A fork is an attack on two or more enemy units by the same piece or pawn at the same time. Forks are most valuable when your opponent is unable to answer both attacks properly. For instance, one of two attacked units moves away but the other one is captured.

The most effective forks are by pawns and knights. A pawn fork is especially dangerous because pawns are less valuable than pieces. If you fork an enemy bishop and knight with a pawn, you win material even if both pieces can be simultaneously protected. It doesn't matter that your opponent can take back. He still loses a piece for a pawn.

Sometimes a forked enemy unit can save itself by capturing the forker. In the case of a forking knight, this is possible only if one of the forked units is itself a knight. No wonder knight forks are so deadly: only another knight can capture the forking knight.

The queen, attacking in all directions, is the most prodigious forker, but due to its great value, it is unable to make many of the captures it threatens because it might be captured in turn.

The most lethal forks involve the enemy king. If the enemy king is attacked, everything else must be put on hold while the king is rescued from check.

If two ordinary units are forked, it is sometimes possible to move one to safety with a gain of tempo, so that on the next move the other forked unit can be saved as well.

By all means, aim to fork your opponent's pieces. Avoid placing your own pieces where they can be forked, especially by pawns and knights.

Gain a Move   Gaining a move and gaining a tempo mean the same thing. Complete an action, sequence, or plan in one less move than thought necessary, and you gain a move. Gain a move and you gain time. Forcing your opponent to squander a move in defense so that you can do something you couldn't otherwise do also gains you time.

In the opening, developing your pieces isn't enough. Always try to develop and threaten simultaneously. If possible, every move should contain a threat. Constantly having to defend against threats ties down your opponent and lets you gain time to carry out your long-range plans.

Hanging Pawns You may have hanging pawns if two of your pawns occupy your fourth rank on adjacent files. True hanging pawns have no enemy pawns blocking the files in front of them and are restrained from moving by enemy pawns and pieces. Such pawns are a liability if the enemy can guard the squares immediately in front of them while attacking the pawns along the half-open files. To ward off such attacks you might have to advance one or both pawns, which exposes them to further risk.

The same pawns, remarkably, can be an asset in slightly different conditions. If the enemy cannot restrain or attack the pawns successfully, and if one of them can become a dangerous passed pawn, you could seize the initiative and develop winning chances.

If you have hanging pawns, support their advance so that you can use them for attack. If your opponent has hanging pawns, restrain their advance and pile up an assault against them. As so often in chess, what counts is how you handle it. If you have these pawns, make them strong. If your opponent has them, make them weak.

Hole A hole is a weak square, often on the third rank, that can't be defended by one's own pawn but is guarded by an enemy pawn, which could protect enemy pieces invading and occupying it. Try to avoid making weakening pawn moves that create holes. If your opponent has incurred such weaknesses, maneuver your own pieces, especially knights, to occupy the hole. Transform the enemy weakness into a strongpoint for you.

Maneuver Maneuvering a piece is repositioning it, usually over the course of at least several moves. Most maneuvers are designed to improve the scope or function of a particular piece or group of pieces.

Since it takes time to transfer pieces across the board, maneuvers are often possible only in closed or semi-closed positions, where the center is blocked and sudden enemy counterattacks are unlikely. If you have the time, try to improve the scope of your pieces by maneuvering them.

Open Game A game is not considered open or partially open unless two central pawns (one for each side) have been exchanged. After the center is at least partly cleared of pawns, it is "open," and movement through the center can proceed with relative ease.

Most traditional chess principles apply mainly to open games: quick and purposeful development, control and occupation of the center, early castling, the immediate seizure of open lines, the fight for the initiative—all are battle cries of the open-game competitor.

Here is where a violation of principle can be punished by a heavy loss of material or a quick mate. The worst villains are unnecessary pawn moves, failure to castle early, moving the queen into battle too early, and wasting time needlessly capturing pawns.

To play successfully, first understand the nature of the position at hand. If the game is open or about to open, rely on open-game principles. Look to attack the enemy king. If the game is closed or semi-closed, play more for position, trying to accumulate small advantages.

Outpost   An outpost is a square on the enemy's third or fourth rank that cannot be protected by one of his pawns and can be occupied by one of your own pieces protected by one of your own pawns guarding that square.

Knights generally are the best outpost occupants, though other pieces often perform well at such fortified points. It helps to have a half-open file leading to your outpost so that your rooks can lend a hand.

Avoid giving your opponent an outpost in your position. Make sure that such potential squares can be protected by one of your pawns. If you have an outpost square, protect it and occupy it with the best piece available.

Pawn Island   Any group of friendly pawns separated from other friendly pawns by at least one file is a pawn island. An island can consist of one or as many as eight pawns. The fewer pawn islands the better, for pawns can more easily defend themselves if they are closer together.

The weakest pawn island of all is the isolated pawn. If your isolated pawn is threatened, it has to be protected by a piece, for no friendly pawns occupy adjacent files. The individual pawns in a larger pawn island can usually draw support from a neighboring pawn, though often at the cost of incurring further weaknesses.

Keep your pawns grouped in as few islands as possible. When you have an opportunity to capture an enemy unit with either of two pawns, choose the capture that gives you the fewest pawn islands. Try to keep your pawns close together unless the demands of the position require you to do otherwise.

Pin   A pin is a tactic that prevents or makes it difficult or unpleasant for an enemy piece or pawn to move off a rank, file, or diagonal. Your piece attacks two enemy units in the same line; the front unit can't move off the line without exposing the unit behind it. If the unit behind it is the enemy king, the pin is absolute, meaning that the front unit cannot legally move. Otherwise the pin is relative; the front unit can move but only by exposing the back one. Your unit "pins" the front enemy unit to the one behind it.

A pin's strategic value can be great. You may not be trying to win an enemy unit at all, but only trying to tie it down to gain time or to immobilize it for defensive reasons.

It's usually a good idea to pin your opponent's pieces and pawns. The pinned unit need not be captured, especially if there's no material gain involved. Instead, keep the enemy unit pinned and take advantage of its trapped position to keep your opponent tied down.

Queenside Majority   If you have more pawns on the queenside (files a through d) than your opponent, you have a queenside majority. When both kings have castled kingside, the queenside majority constitutes a positional advantage.

Especially in the endgame, mobilize your majority to create a passed pawn, and use it to decoy the enemy king to the queenside, so that the enemy kingside is vulnerable to your king and other pieces.

In the middlegame, a queenside majority can be used as the basis of a queenside attack. The object is not the enemy king, which is on the kingside, but the enemy pawns and weak squares. Sometimes, particularly in open positions, you can advance your queenside majority for an attack there, and then, when enemy forces have been diverted to the queenside, switch to the kingside to get at the enemy king. This works if your mobility is good and the enemy pieces out of position.

Sacrifice   A sacrifice is a voluntary surrender of material for attack or positional considerations. If the advantage to be gained by giving up material is clear and immediate, that sacrifice is merely a gesture, a "sham" or "pseudo" sacrifice. If the consequences of the sacrifice are unclear and risky, it is a real sacrifice.

There are plenty of tactical reasons for offering real sacrifices, but strategic ones can be important, too. You might sacrifice to trap your opponent's king in the center, to inhibit his development, to demolish his pawn structure, to induce weaknesses, and so on.

As a training exercise, try making reasonable sacrifices in every game, at least while developing your attacking skills. Being behind in material will force you to play harder and more creatively. The quality of your overall game must thereby improve.

Seventh Rank   Here's where you find the meat and potatoes. Once you have control of an open file (with your rook on it unopposed by an enemy rook), try to move your rook safely to the seventh rank. You will probably thus be placing several enemy pawns in jeopardy, as well as threatening the enemy king. A rook on the seventh is a great advantage in the endgame, and in the middlegame is a part of an attack on the enemy king. Two rooks on the seventh are usually decisive.

Transposition   One position is a transposition of another if it is the same position reached by a different move order. The change in move order is often insignificant and of no advantage one way or the other. But sometimes the different order is critical and can give you the upper hand.

By varying the move order you might force your opponent to make a concession, defend, or waste time instead of developing or continuing with his own plans. The forfeit of a single move could permanently disrupt your opponent's natural strategy.

A clever transposition also might fool your opponent. You might have a pet variation that your opponent is aware of and tries to avoid. If you are able to change the move order, he might not realize what you have in mind. He might think you're planning one thing and get set up for that contingency, when a surprise twist or resource brings matters back to your original intention. Meanwhile, having failed to anticipate this possibility, he is out of position.

In an opening, study the key positions and the different ways to achieve them. Games will develop where you might have to take the back road if the main highway is blocked.

Zugzwang   This German word means "compulsion to move." In the endgame, you are "in zugzwang" when any move you make loses or worsens your game.

Zugzwang is rarely a factor in the middlegame; unless you are facing certain mate, there are probably a number of moves that won't worsen your position. Don't count on putting your opponent in a middlegame zugzwang, but, as a general policy, you should try to restrict his play and reduce his options.

INDEX

♟ ♜ ♟